LEON SCHREIBER

COALITION
COUNTRY

South Africa after the ANC

TAFELBERG

Tafelberg
An imprint of NB Publishers, a Division of Media24 Boeke (Pty) Ltd
40 Heerengracht, Cape Town
www.tafelberg.com

Text © Leon Schreiber (2018)
Cover images © Ramaphosa: Linda Mthombeni/GCIS,
Malema and Maimane: Gallo Images

Cover design: Gaelen Pinnock | www.scarletstudio.net
Book design: Nazli Jacobs
Editing: Riaan de Villiers
Proofreading: Kelly Norwood-Young
Index: Sanet le Roux

solutions
Printed by **novus print**, a Novus Holdings company

First edition, first impression 2018

ISBN: 978-0-624-08394-8
Epub: 978-0-624-08395-5
Mobi: 978-0-624-08396-2

For Julia,

who makes the future worth imagining

Table of contents

Introduction

Two decades from now, it will seem almost absurd that South African politics was once totally dominated by the African National Congress (ANC). The current reality, with the ANC holding overwhelming power at the national, provincial and municipal levels, will seem just as foreign to the next generation as the idea of a white minority government to most South Africans today. By then, our political system will be fundamentally different; South Africa will be governed by coalitions, with no single party holding more than 50 per cent of the vote.

Jacob Zuma will be remembered not only as a megalomaniac whose greed brought the country to the brink of collapse, but also as an example of how absolute power corrupts absolutely. In one of the most culturally diverse societies on earth, and with dozens of different political coalitions in charge across the country, history students in the year 2038 will marvel at the hubris of Zuma's 2014 prediction that the ANC will 'run this government forever and ever . . . until Jesus comes back'.[1]

The ANC won't disappear. However, it will soon lose its iron grip on the country's politics, with ANC single-party governments replaced by a broad range of political coalitions. Travelling across this vast and beautiful country, the next generation of South Africans will encounter radically different governments from one municipality and province to another, while no single party will have absolute power at the national level. The history class of

2038 might well look back at the 2019 national and provincial elections as the turning point that put South Africa firmly on the path to coalition politics.

The debate that dominated South African public life in the build-up to the ANC's 54th national elective conference, held in Johannesburg on 16–20 December 2017, was symptomatic of a country that has been psychologically colonised by one-party domination. In the weeks leading up to the event, everyone, from stockbrokers and bankers to farmers and construction workers, were held in thrall by the prospect of the ANC electing a new leader to replace the corrupt and destructive Jacob Zuma.

Like the ocean tides following the cycles of the moon, the South African rand rose and fell in response to speculation about whether billionaire businessman Cyril Ramaphosa would emerge victorious from the conference, or whether Zuma's ex-wife, Nkosazana Dlamini-Zuma, would walk away with the dubious honour of becoming the next leader of the corrupt gang that the ANC had become.

In the days following the news that Ramaphosa had won the party's internal leadership contest, the rand rose to a two-and-a-half-year high.[2] This was despite the fact that the ANC had also officially adopted populist policies like the nationalisation of the Reserve Bank and the expropriation of commercial farmland without compensation, which would – if implemented – drop a nuclear bomb on South Africa's financial system. After the conference, Ramaphosa's cheerleaders also declared that he was about to rid the party of corruption, even though the ANC is entirely fuelled by it, and despite the fact that he would have to contend with an internal leadership packed with Zuma's fellow trough-feeders.

Why exactly is it that South Africans from all walks of life were so obsessed with the ANC's elective conference? After all, the country is nominally a multiparty democracy, so why pay so much attention to – and bet so much money on – the internal manoeuvres of a single political party? The answer is that, for the past two-and-a-half decades, every political discussion in South Africa has been almost entirely premised on one central assumption: that the ANC, and the ANC alone, would continue to govern this country.

Therefore, Jacob Zuma is not the only one who believes the ANC will run South Africa 'until Jesus comes back'. Whether they support the party or not, almost all South Africans share his belief that the ANC will be in power for the foreseeable future. Even ardent opposition supporters will admit that the idea of the ANC losing national power has always been more of a pipe dream than a tangible goal. Most South Africans simply cannot imagine their country without the ANC in charge. It really is extraordinary that the party has been so dominant since coming to power in 1994 that it even holds sway over the imaginations of those who despise it.

Zuma in fact perfectly illustrated the belief in the ANC's invincibility when he reportedly burst out laughing after his party had lost its majorities in Nelson Mandela Bay, Johannesburg and Tshwane in the 2016 local elections.[3] That Zuma can laugh in the face of such a defeat not only attests to his arrogance, but also the inability to imagine the ANC ever losing an important election. The assumption that the party will be in power 'forever' is so deeply engrained in the South African psyche that it goes almost entirely unexamined.

In contrast, in consolidated democracies where power changes hands regularly, the levels of excitement and intrigue that accompanied the ANC's national elective conference is only reserved for multiparty elections. But in South Africa, the ANC's near-complete dominance means that the outcomes of the party's internal contests have become more important than those of actual elections involving different political parties. Since 1994, citizens have thus correctly assumed that whoever becomes ANC president will almost automatically become the country's president.

But this is *not* inevitable. Despite the ANC's dominance, South Africa remains an electoral democracy, where multiparty polls are the real determinant of who becomes the next president. This book shows that, for the first time since 1994, there is no guarantee that ANC president Ramaphosa will automatically become the South African president. Given the party's rapid downward slide, it is high time for all citizens to start imagining a future without the ANC in outright control of the country.

In practice, this means that the financial traders who are relieved and enthused by Ramaphosa's internal victory should not count their chickens before they hatch. Instead of assuming that the supposedly business-friendly Ramaphosa will easily win the 2019 national election, financial sector professionals should invest in serious planning for the possibility of the ANC losing that election. To use an investment metaphor: it would be dangerous simply to extrapolate the ANC's past electoral returns into the future.

Equally, farmers and the millions of citizens who are anxious about the ANC's plan to grab farmland and other property should keep in mind that it is no longer 1994, and that the party's loss of moral authority puts it on a path to be out of power soon, meaning that those destructive plans may remain on paper only. The same goes for every other industry and citizen in the country who has thus far merely assumed that because the ANC was dominant in the past, it will remain dominant in the future.

But with our democracy having grown up in a state of one-party domination, imagining a South Africa devoid of ANC hegemony is easier said than done. What, exactly, should we be planning for if the ANC gets less than 50 per cent of the vote in 2019?

This book seeks to answer this question by showing why South Africa is on the cusp of another great transformation, in which coalition politics will move to the centre of our national life once the ANC loses its dominant position. It not only documents the rapid and ongoing decline of the once all-conquering ANC, but also shows how and why South Africa's electoral system favours coalitions over single-party governments, and why none of the current opposition parties will soon be able to garner majorities on their own.

It also examines coalition best practice elsewhere in the world, and explores what different coalition configurations are likely to mean for the country. What would a national DA-EFF government, ANC-EFF government, or minority government look like? What compromises could they strike, and what policies are they likely to implement?

By opening a conversation about the dramatic changes that could accompany the dawn of the coalition era, this book seeks to illuminate the path towards imagining a South Africa in which vibrant – if sometimes chaotic – multiparty politics replaces the stale domination of single-party rule.

PART ONE
Why coalitions are coming

Chapter One

Getting to grips with our coalition future

A powerful exception

The ANC has governed South Africa for more than two decades – a long time for any one party to be in power on its own in a multiparty democracy. In fact, only three of the world's 79 democracies – Botswana, Malaysia and Namibia[1] – currently have a governing party that governed on its own for longer than the ANC.

The ANC's dominance is reflected in the national election results. In South Africa's first democratic election on 27 April 1994, the ANC, then led by Nelson Mandela, won 62.65 per cent of the vote.[2] This increased to 66.35 per cent in 1999, when Thabo Mbeki became president, followed by 69.69 per cent, at the start of Mbeki's second term, in 2004. This meant that, from 2004 to 2009, the ANC controlled more than two thirds of the seats in the National Assembly, giving the party enough power to change the Constitution on its own. This is likely to go down in history as the high-water mark of single-party hegemony. ANC support slightly declined to 65.90 per cent in 2009, with Zuma poised to become president, followed by a further drop to 62.15 per cent in 2014.

For more than two decades, the ANC has controlled not only

the national government, but also at least seven out of nine provinces, and more than 90 per cent of municipalities. Since the end of apartheid, South Africa has been a single-party regime in which it has been hard to imagine the ANC losing a national election.

But the story of single-party dominance actually started long before the ANC got into power. The ANC's near-complete control since 1994 was preceded by 46 years of one-party rule under the whites-only National Party (NP).[3] In fact, under the NP and ANC, South Africa has experienced 70 years of uninterrupted single-party governance.

As a result, South Africans are used to one party calling the shots. We expect most cabinet ministers to belong to a single dominant party, and we are used to having a Parliament in which 'party discipline' is enough to ensure that any legislation the ruling party wants is passed without much difficulty. Analysts and observers are also accustomed to blaming corruption and the ANC's many governance failures on the fact that its dominance is not under threat, and there is thus little incentive for it to govern well.[4] As with the once all-conquering NP, the ANC's dominance has bred arrogance, poor governance, and contempt for South African citizens.

A fading hegemon

But current electoral trends suggest that the ANC's remarkable run is coming to an end. A combination of endemic corruption, rising crime, a stalled economy, and the party's staunch defence of Zuma's patronage network has gradually eroded its support since 2009, and since 2014 this trend has rapidly accelerated.

Figure 1 outlines electoral trends in national and municipal elections from 1994 to 2016, and projects those trends into the future to the 2019 national and provincial elections and the municipal elections in 2021.[5] The key takeaway is that, for the first time in 25 years, the ANC may lose its majority in the next national and provincial elections.

Figure 1: ANC and opposition votes in national and municipal elections, 1994–2021 (actual and projected)

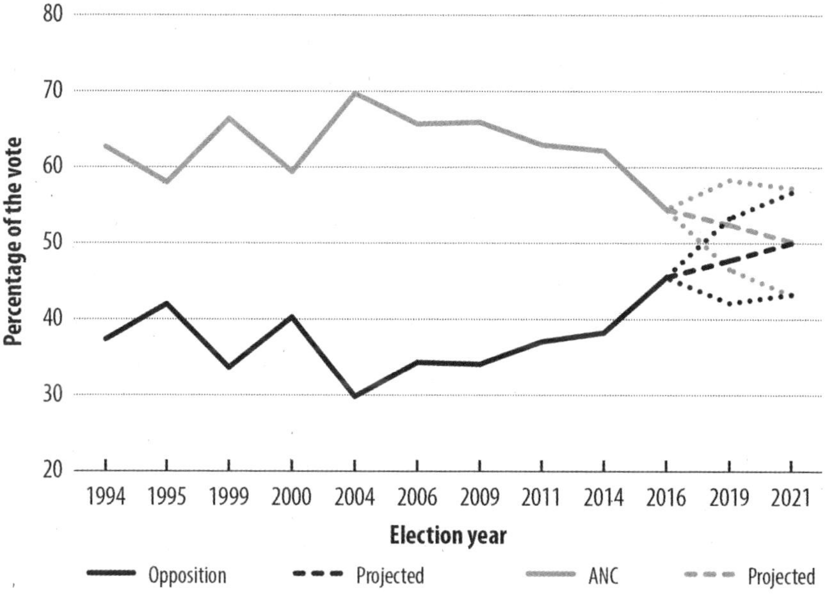

Source: Electoral Commission of South Africa.

While earlier efforts to imagine a post-ANC future were largely premised on wishful thinking, the data shows that the time has arrived for South Africans to start imagining what the country's politics will be like without the dominance of a single party. As Chapter Two will show, the ANC is also in big trouble when it comes to many urban municipalities as well as at the provincial level in the Western Cape, Gauteng, and even North West and the Northern Cape provinces.

19

Now that it is no longer a foregone conclusion that the ANC will win all upcoming municipal, provincial and national elections, we need to ask the most important question of our time: what will rise when the ANC falls? The answer is that, based on the country's proportional representation electoral system, the ANC will be replaced not by another single party but by a coalition of political parties. When the two lines in Figure 1 cross, national coalitions will become the default form of government in South Africa.

The purpose of this book is to explore the far-reaching implications of the imminent shift to coalition governance. It is a shift that will force different groups to co-operate and compromise. This will transform South Africa's political landscape, and the consequences will be felt by everyone.

We should briefly mention the ANC's long-standing collaboration with the South African Communist Party (SACP) and the Congress of South African Trade Unions (Cosatu). Although the ANC, SACP and Cosatu refer to themselves as a 'tripartite alliance', until 2017, no South African had ever cast an electoral vote for the SACP or Cosatu. (In November 2017, for the first time ever, the SACP fielded its own candidates in a by-election in the northern Free State municipality of Metsimaholo – Chapter Two returns to this remarkable break with the past). Rather than being proper coalition partners of the ANC, the SACP and Cosatu have thus far merely represented different factions within the ANC. Unlike the tripartite alliance, South Africa will soon have true, democratically elected coalition governments where all coalition partners will have to answer directly to voters.

A permanent Codesa

During the multiparty negotiations at the Convention for a Democratic South Africa (Codesa) in the early 1990s, political leaders and ordinary South Africans alike demonstrated that they were capable of averting a race war, and fostering mutually beneficial outcomes through negotiation and compromise. The success of the Codesa negotiations in producing a democratic dispensation made such a big impression on the national psyche that, during the ensuing decades, political and civic leaders have repeatedly argued that only a 'new Codesa' could address South Africa's persistent social and economic problems.

They may soon get a version of what they wished for. With coalitions set to become the default mode of government from as early as 2019, South Africans will soon be governed by a permanent Codesa in which different political parties are forced to work together.

It is no accident that coalitions will rise when ANC domination falls. During the multiparty negotiations in the early 1990s, leaders from across the political spectrum deliberately designed an electoral system that would encourage coalition governments. Even before formal negotiations over the electoral system began in 1993, there was already near-total agreement between the ANC, NP and the Democratic Party (DP) that a coalition-based electoral system – known as proportional representation – was the way to go. Let's revisit their reasoning.

In 1993, the ANC's constitutional specialist, Kader Asmal, declared that South Africa's cultural, social and economic diversity required an electoral system at all levels that would 'enable sectoral groups to be adequately represented in decision-making'.[6]

21

Given the need to ensure that as many political parties as possible would be represented in Parliament, the drafters of the Constitution chose proportional representation over the main alternative, a winner-take-all system (sometimes also called first-past-the-post).

While winner-take-all systems are arguably more stable because they usually do not require coalitions, Asmal and his associates from different parties explicitly rejected that option because of its tendency to produce governments that do not fully represent all voices in society.[7] Under winner-take-all, it is easy for one party to control the national government even with less than half of the national vote. Winner-take-all is a zero-sum game: either your party's candidate wins, or you have no voice in the legislature or executive. Given the low level of representation inherent to winner-take-all systems, both the interim and final Constitutions eventually stated that the composition of the National Assembly – the lower house of Parliament – should result 'in general, in proportional representation'.[8] With this short phrase, proportional representation became the cornerstone of South Africa's entire political system.

This decision was based on the desire of the Constitution's architects to create a 'new South Africa' in which inter-group conflict would be superseded by co-operation and compromise. As the term suggests, proportional representation is primarily concerned with ensuring that election outcomes mirror the preferences expressed by *all* voters – not just by the majority of voters, or even by a majority of a minority. It does this by assigning seats in Parliament in direct proportion to the number of votes any party gets.

In fact, under South Africa's proportional representation system, any party that wins as little as 0.25 per cent of the national vote will get at least one seat in Parliament. (In the 2014 election, this meant that a party needed only about 45 000 votes to get a single seat.) This is the lowest threshold possible under any electoral framework.[9] The system's inclusivity contrasts starkly with the exclusionary outcomes in winner-take-all countries such as Britain or the United States, and ensures that no one's vote is wasted.

In South Africa, if party A wins 40 per cent of the national vote, it gets 160 of the 400 seats in the National Assembly. If party B wins 35 per cent of the nationwide vote, it gets exactly 140 seats, while 25 per cent for party C would guarantee it 100 seats. Unlike winner-take-all, proportional representation turns elections into positive-sum games: one party's victory does not automatically mean that other parties do not make it into Parliament (or into government). It is easy to see why this system is better suited to plural and diverse societies such as South Africa.

But the real power of the proportional representation model kicks in when no party wins more than 50 per cent of the national vote. Let's assume that the ANC dips just below 50 per cent in the 2019 national election, while the Democratic Alliance (DA), the Economic Freedom Fighters (EFF), and other opposition parties marginally increasing their shares of the vote. For the first time in post-apartheid South Africa, no single party would be able to form a national government without the support of at least one other party.

This is because the crucial step in forming a government is when the National Assembly elects one of its members as president, who then proceeds to appoint a cabinet. For this to happen, someone needs the support of at least 201 of the 400 MPs. Since 1994, the election of the president has always been a mere formality, as the ANC never had fewer than 249 MPs. But once the party's share of the popular vote drops below 50 per cent, the ANC will have less than the required 201 seats in the National Assembly. This is the moment when coalitions will move to the epicentre of national politics. When ANC support drops below 50 per cent, any combination of parties will be free to form a government as long as they are able to get 201 MPs to vote for their preferred presidential candidate.

Even if the ANC was still the largest party – even if it had 199 seats, and its closest competitor only had 120 – it would still be out of power if opposition parties managed to form a coalition that added together all of their 201 seats. However, the ANC would remain in power if it managed to convince a party with just two seats to join it in a coalition, and support its presidential candidate.

The rule is simple: whichever party's candidate gets 201 or more votes becomes president. The president then appoints a deputy president, ministers, and deputy ministers to his or her cabinet, thereby formally assembling a government.

Once coalitions become the norm, seemingly minor political parties will suddenly begin to play tremendously important roles. In the above scenario, the ANC would need to convince a minority party with only two Parliamentary seats (equal to only 0.5 per cent of the vote, or about 90 000 votes) to join it in a coalition. This means that the two parties would need to strike a deal. Based on experiences in other countries governed by coalitions, such a deal usually entails that the junior partner gets a few important portfolios, like foreign affairs or even the deputy presidency. The senior partner will generally also have to agree to some policy concessions to convince the smaller party to join it. This means that parties representing minority interests, such as the African Christian Democratic Party (ACDP) or the Freedom Front Plus (FF+), could soon play an important role in governing South Africa.

But there is another potential outcome. If no group of parties in the National Assembly is able to cobble together a formal alliance that would take them over the 201-seat mark, the country could get a so-called minority government. Similar to what happened in Johannesburg and Tshwane after the 2016 municipal election, a group of parties may agree to support the same candidate for president without constituting a formal coalition.

The proportional representation system therefore precisely reflects the will of the voters, even if their will is that no one party should have enough power to form a government on its own. In a plural society like ours, proportional representation will soon lead to a fractured political landscape in which it will be very difficult for any one party to get consistent majorities.

Defying destiny

But this prediction also raises an obvious question: if South Africa's electoral framework encourages coalitions, why has the ANC been able to rule on its own since 1994? Indeed, in countries with proportional representation systems, coalition governments are the rule, and one-party majorities the rare exceptions. This makes the ANC's two decades of domination even more impressive, as its majorities were not artificially inflated by the vagaries of winner-take-all. Instead, the opposite happened – the ANC achieved its majorities in a system explicitly designed to encourage plurality and coalition governance.

The ANC's dominance since 1994 is a powerful illustration that although rules and structures favour certain outcomes over others (in this case, coalition rather than majoritarian government), they are never enough to *guarantee* that those outcomes will materialise. Although the rules of our electoral system favour multiparty coalitions over single-party majorities, democracy means that those rules are not absolute. They can be overridden wherever voters strongly prefer a single party.

This is precisely what happened during South Africa's first two-and-a-half decades of democracy, as the ANC's liberation narrative proved powerful enough to overcome the logic of the electoral system. The ANC was so overwhelmingly popular that it was able to engineer single-party rule in an environment that actively discouraged it.

But once the power of the ANC's liberation narrative is sufficiently weakened, and its mighty majorities vanish, South African politics will be transformed. This will be no accident, as the proportional representation of every cultural, ethnic and political group, as well as forced coalitions among them, is precisely what constitutional framers from opposite ends of the political spectrum envisioned when they wrote the rules in the mid-1990s.

The ANC's ability to overcome the tendency towards coalitions meant that citizens wrongly became used to the idea that South African democracy entails clear and unbending distinctions between one powerful governing party and an amalgam of minor opposition parties nipping at the ANC's heels. One indication of this perception is audible whenever someone speaks of the ANC as a 'ruling' party.

This term has authoritarian overtones; it may be appropriate to describe a dictator as a 'ruler', but a democratically elected government does not rule over its citizens. It governs on their behalf. That 'ruling party' instead of 'governing party' has become the default way to describe the ANC in public discussions says a lot about South Africans' perception of the party as an all-powerful entity capable of enforcing its will. The widespread use of the authoritarian-sounding 'ruling party' is not a trivial detail: it shows how South Africans have come to regard the exceptional situation of single-party dominance as the norm.

This perception of the ANC will soon come crashing down. While the party has thus far used its powerful history to thwart the electoral system's tendency towards coalitions, its fast declining electoral fortunes means this domination is in its death throes. In its place, coalition governments will rise.

Roadmap to the future

This book's analysis of our coalition future proceeds from three assumptions. The first is that the trend outlined in Figure 1 is set to continue – in other words, that the ANC's electoral decline will not be arrested in the short term. This means it will become increasingly difficult for the party to garner majorities in metropolitan municipalities like Tshwane, Johannesburg, Ekurhuleni and Nelson Mandela Bay, as well as in larger rural centres like Rustenburg and Polokwane. The result is that, at the municipal level, the ANC will increasingly resemble a rural-based party, while urban competitors like the DA and EFF will continue to make inroads in the cities.

This bottom-up process of change is currently accelerating to the point where the ANC will soon lose its majority in the urbanised province of Gauteng, while the Western Cape will remain out of its reach. Its winning margins in other provinces will also decline, with North West and the Northern Cape perhaps third and fourth in line to fall. (Dissatisfaction of Zuma loyalists with Ramaphosa means that even KwaZulu-Natal might soon be up for grabs.) As soon as 2019, this trend could culminate in the ANC losing its majority in a national election. With no party able to muster 50 per cent of the national vote, this will mark the final death knell of single-party domination in South Africa. However, this does not imply that the ANC will fade from the political scene. Even in South Africa's approaching coalition future, the ANC is likely to remain the single biggest political force. But it will no longer be near-invincible.

Could another political party replace the ANC as a dominant force that controls the national government as well as most of the country's provinces and municipalities? This points to our second assumption, namely that the end of ANC majorities will probably mean the beginning of no majorities. Despite the fact that the EFF in particular likes to talk about itself as a 'government in waiting'[10] – and despite media coverage that often portrays electoral choices as either/or scenarios – neither the EFF, DA, or any other party will become dominant once the ANC falls below 50 per cent.

Instead, we will soon have dozens of situations where, for example, a local municipality is governed by the DA in coalition with the EFF and an independent councillor, while the surrounding district municipality may be controlled by an ANC-Congress of the People (COPE) coalition. In turn, both of those municipalities might be nestled within a province run by a coalition between the DA, the United Democratic Movement (UDM) and the FF+, while a coalition comprising the ANC, the National Freedom Party (NFP) and the ACDP could be in control at the national level. To survive and thrive in our coalition future, we must urgently prepare to deal with a scale of political complexity we have never seen or experienced before.

The third assumption is the most fundamental, as it presumes that elections will remain free and fair, and that the ANC will remain willing to give up power where and when its dominant majorities disappear. As regards the fairness of elections, the Electoral Commission of South Africa (IEC) has been widely praised for its competent administration of the electoral process.[11] But a recent ruling by the Constitutional Court exposed the fact that the IEC had failed to capture the addresses of up to 16 million of the 24 million voters on the national voters' roll. In June 2016, the court gave the IEC 18 months to make sure that all voters' address details were correctly captured on the voters' roll.[12] For our election results to remain credible, the IEC must urgently repair the damage.

But even if our elections remain free and fair, it is still not a given that the ANC – used to being in near-total control of South African politics – would accept defeat at the polls, particularly at the national level. On the one hand, there are some encouraging signs. Even though the party branded the DA's 2009 victory in the Western Cape as a triumph for 'racists', and referred to its main opposition as 'the enemy', the ANC did accept defeat.[13] Even more significant was the relatively peaceful transfer of power from the ANC to opposition parties in the major municipalities of Johannesburg, Tshwane and Nelson Mandela Bay after the

2016 local elections.

However, there have also been worrying indications that the party will not always be gracious in defeat. In the Western Cape, a few years ago, some ANC leaders declared in public that the ANC would seek to make the province 'ungovernable', with the aim of unseating the DA. (These declarations only abated when Helen Zille, provincial premier and then leader of the DA, pointed out that these statements constituted a prima facie instance of sedition, and criminal charges were laid against ANC Youth League leaders.)[14] In all three big cities the ANC lost in 2016, ANC councillors have also been involved in periodic violent skirmishes against the new leadership.[15]

Finally, and most disturbingly, the run-up to the 2016 municipal election was marred by a spate of political assassinations in KwaZulu-Natal and Gauteng,[16] and another wave of killings broke out in KwaZulu-Natal in 2017. These served as a warning that some ANC functionaries were willing to kill to hold on to power. One can only hope that this murderous tendency does not serve as harbinger of the ANC's attitude to electoral defeat.

If these three assumptions hold up – that the ANC's decline will continue, that no opposition party will become dominant, and that elections will remain free and fair – coalition politics is guaranteed to emerge as the new *leitmotiv* for South African society. The rest of this book grapples with the implications. It is divided into three parts. The first part explains *why* it is only now, after more than two decades of democracy, that coalitions are set to become the default form of government. The second part explores *what* coalitions are likely to mean via three coalition scenarios. Finally, the third part looks at practical examples of *how* to make coalitions work.

Even if the ANC manages to sneak above the 50 per cent mark in 2019, its fast declining fortunes (as discussed in Chapter Two) make it clear that the era of one-party dominance is coming to an end. The simple reality is that the ANC will not remain in power forever – neither at the municipal, provincial nor national level. This book argues that the turning point at the national level will probably come in 2019, but the exact date of the ANC's fall is less important than the fact that coalitions will soon become the default form of government in South Africa. Whether the ANC loses its national majority in 2019 or 2024, the key point is that wherever the party loses an election, it will likely be replaced by a coalition government. South Africans must urgently start preparing for this new reality.

Chapter Two

The decline of the ANC

Wednesday 3 August 2016, the day of the fifth round of municipal elections after South Africa's transition to democracy, was a watershed in the country's political history. Although some preceding by-elections had showed that electoral support for the ANC was declining, there was little concrete evidence that large numbers of ANC voters would ever abstain, or vote for any other political party. But on that fateful day in the winter of 2016, the first chinks in the ANC's armour began to show.

The first sign that the ANC's support was plummeting came in Cape Town, a bastion of opposition politics after the ANC's defeat in the municipal elections in 2006. On the Thursday morning after the elections, Capetonians woke to the news that the DA was on its way to securing an overwhelming majority. By midday, it was all but confirmed: the DA had won 66.61 per cent of the Cape Town vote – the highest voting share ever achieved by any party in that city.

By the Friday, it was clear that the ANC had also been roundly defeated in the rest of the Western Cape, where it had only managed to get more votes than the DA in two out of 29 district and local municipalities. The ANC might have reasoned that, while the Western Cape results were unfortunate, they were not entirely unexpected. There was still hope that the damage might be limited to one province.

On Friday afternoon, though, those hopes were shattered when the IEC confirmed that the ANC had also lost Nelson Mandela Bay, home to Port Elizabeth, a major port and the Eastern Cape's biggest city. It was a momentous defeat for the ANC in its traditional regional heartland. Defeat would have been unthinkable as recently as 2006, when the ANC won Nelson Mandela Bay with 67.61 per cent of the vote. Now, it could only muster 41.50 per cent. By contrast, the DA vote had swelled from 24.14 per cent in 2006 to 46.66 per cent. The convenor of the ANC's Eastern Cape electoral task team, Beza Ntshona, conceded that this was a 'painful' blow in the home of the ANC, where, 'for the first time since the dawn of democracy, the ANC has not won'.[1]

By the weekend, the nation's attention was focused on Gauteng, scene of an epic battle for control of Pretoria, South Africa's administrative capital, and Johannesburg, its most economically significant city. At midday on Saturday 6 August, the IEC announced that the DA had taken Tshwane. It had garnered 43.10 per cent of the vote, up from 30.70 per cent in 2006, while the ANC vote had declined to 41.48 per cent from 57.32 per cent a decade earlier. The DA forged a coalition with the ACDP, COPE and the FF+, with support from the EFF, which took control of the capital city.[2]

But the ANC's most significant defeat came in Johannesburg, where it lost control of the metro despite obtaining 44.50 per cent of the vote – nearly six per cent more than the DA. Because

South Africa's electoral system requires a majority of 50 per cent plus one in a municipal council, the DA was able to forge a coalition with the ACDP, COPE, FF+, UDM and IFP, again with support from the EFF, to take charge of Johannesburg as well. On 22 August 2016, the DA's mayoral candidate, Herman Mashaba, became the first post-1994 mayor of South Africa's biggest and economically most important city who did not carry an ANC membership card.

A municipal revolution

When the dust settled, it emerged that the ANC had lost control of four of South Africa's eight big metropolitan areas (or 'metropolitan municipalities') – Cape Town, Nelson Mandela Bay, Tshwane and Johannesburg. It is hard to overstate the significance of its defeat in the latter two. The combined economy of Pretoria and Johannesburg is bigger than the economies of all but four African countries. Although the ANC retained power in three other metros (Buffalo City, eThekwini and Mangaung) and formed a governing coalition council in a fourth (Ekurhuleni), the party's combined support in the eight metros had declined by more than 10 per cent since 2011.

Most significantly, four (Nelson Mandela Bay, Johannesburg, Tshwane and Ekurhuleni) of the eight metros are now governed by either majority or minority coalitions. The trend is clear: at the local level, the ANC's support is rapidly declining and – based on electoral trends since 2006 – will continue to decline for the foreseeable future (see Figure 2). Conversely, the likelihood of metropolitan municipalities being run by coalitions is increasing.

Nationwide, the ANC's support across all municipalities fell by more than 8 per cent between 2011 and 2016 to 54.49 per cent.

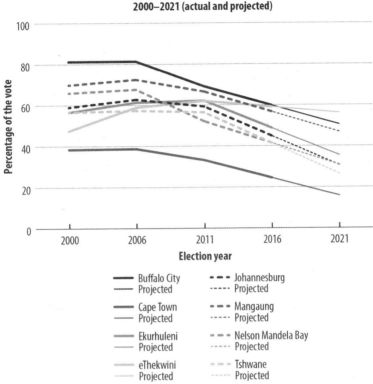

Figure 2: ANC vote in SA's eight metropolitan municipalities, 2000–2021 (actual and projected)

━━━ Buffalo City	▪ ▪ ▪ Johannesburg
─── Projected	----- Projected
━━━ Cape Town	▪ ▪ ▪ Mangaung
─── Projected	----- Projected
━━━ Ekurhuleni	▪ ▪ ▪ Nelson Mandela Bay
─── Projected	----- Projected
━━━ eThekwini	═ ═ ═ Tshwane
─── Projected	----- Projected

Source: Electoral Commission of South Africa.

The ANC's losses in Cape Town, Nelson Mandela Bay, Tshwane and Johannesburg, as well as in a handful of rural municipalities, signalled a fundamental shift in the country's municipal politics. Up to the 2016 elections, the ANC had controlled 82.10 per cent of South Africa's R287 billion municipal operating budget (the budget used to pay salaries and other regular expenses). Now, its share of the budget had dropped by a staggering R116 billion to only 41.73 per cent.[3] At the same time, the share of the municipal budget controlled by municipalities where the DA was in

35

outright control had increased from 14.95 per cent in 2011 to 15.63 per cent.[4]

So where did the rest of the money go? Crucially, after the 2016 elections, the share of municipal operating funds managed by councils run by coalition governments shot up from just 2.63 per cent in 2011 to a massive 41.31 per cent.[5] In other words, municipalities governed by coalitions – whether formal, such as the DA-led multiparty coalition in Nelson Mandela Bay, or the minority coalitions supported by the EFF in Johannesburg and Tshwane – now control about R118 billion in municipal public funds.

The amount of money controlled by non-ANC municipal councils now roughly equals the combined budgets of all ANC-led municipalities. To underscore the ANC's fall from municipal grace: following the 2016 elections, 58.27 per cent of South Africa's local government budget is *not* controlled by the party.

Accelerating decline

A gradual trend away from one-party dominance is also visible at the provincial and national levels. At the provincial level, the ANC seems set to lose power in at least the Western Cape and Gauteng, which together account for half of South Africa's total economic output (and provincial budgets). After the 2019 elections, the share of provincial government budgets controlled by non-ANC coalitions will probably be at least as great as the share controlled by the ANC.

The national trend is equally pronounced. While the ANC's support seems to have remained remarkably stable between 1994 and 2014, hovering between a high of 69.60 per cent and a low of

62.15 per cent, we need to note that the most recent national data come from 2014. There is ample evidence that the party's support has declined significantly since then, as the Zuma administration has lurched from one scandal to another. Although it can be misleading to draw firm conclusions from comparing different types of elections, it is still useful to include, alongside the national results, a national rollup from municipal elections.[6] Figure 3 reflects the results of a statistical model in which national and provincial electoral trends from 1994 to 2016 are projected up to 2021. It shows that support for the ANC could drop below 50 per cent as early as 2019.

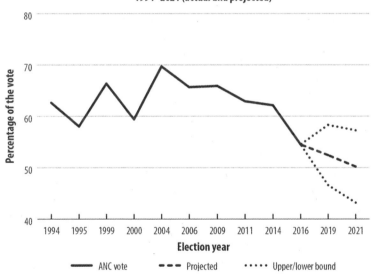

Figure 3: ANC share of the national and municipal vote, 1994–2021 (actual and projected)

Source: Electoral Commission of South Africa.

Another indication that the ANC is in trouble at the national level comes from public opinion polls, which have consistently shown growing dissatisfaction with the ANC-led national government since 2009. In a poll conducted in March 2017, Ipsos found that 53 per cent of South African adults felt the country was moving in the 'wrong' direction (another 16 per cent were undecided, while only 31 per cent were satisfied). Significantly, there was almost no difference between the number of dissatisfied people who received social grants (51 per cent) and those who did not (53 per cent).[7]

The polls show that dissatisfaction cuts across economic divides, bolstering the notion that the ANC is facing an electoral revolt. The most authoritative proof comes from Afrobarometer, a pan-African research network that publishes public opinion polls on a wide range of topics related to democratic governance. In its most recent poll, Afrobarometer found that South Africans' overall trust in the ANC had plummeted from 61 per cent in 2011 to 43 per cent in late 2015 – a massive 18 per cent.[8] Another Ipsos poll conducted in May 2017 found that 65 per cent of South Africans (and 54 per cent of ANC supporters) wanted Zuma to resign as president. At 2.8 out of 10, Zuma's presidential approval rating was the lowest recorded since polling began in 1993.[9]

Nonetheless, disapproval of the Zuma administration may not automatically translate into abstentions, or votes against the ANC. But this is where the 2016 municipal results become even more significant, as they provide the first solid evidence that ANC voters are changing their voting behaviour in order to register their dissatisfaction with the party. Before 3 August 2016, no one could definitively say that a significant number of ANC supporters would ever abstain en masse, or vote for someone else. But they did, and now we can. While trends can be misleading, and it can be risky to project municipal election results onto the provincial and national level, it seems at least clear that the ANC's national support will not increase in 2019. This means it is almost certain to decline – the only question is by how much.

An interesting hint appears when we compare municipal results with national ones. Between 1994 and 2009, the ANC's results at different electoral levels moved in a narrow band – its national results were about 8 per cent to 10 per cent better than its results in the preceding municipal elections. For example, while the party received 59.92 per cent of all votes in the 2000 municipal elections, this increased to 69.69 per cent in the 2004 national poll. But this pattern ended abruptly in 2009 when Zuma became president, as the ANC barely improved on its total in the preceding municipal elections. What's more, in the 2014 national and provincial elections, the ANC vote actually *declined* by 0.78 per cent compared to its vote in the 2011 municipal elections – a telling reverse of the trend during its first 15 years in power.

This shows that the ANC will soon be in big trouble. In the 2016 municipal elections, the ANC vote dropped to an all-time low of 54.49 per cent.[10] If the recent trend – with the ANC failing to increase its vote in national elections relative to municipal elections – persists, its share of the vote in the 2019 national and provincial elections will be smaller, and could even drop to below 50 per cent of the total.

This likelihood grows when one digs a little deeper into the national and provincial results. Even if the ANC 'only' loses the Western Cape (26.83 per cent in 2016) and Gauteng (46.38 per cent in 2016), this may already be enough to push its national support below 50 per cent. This is because more than one of every three South African voters lives in one of these two provinces.

If the ANC is hammered in the Western Cape and Gauteng, and its support drops only marginally in the rest of the country, it will be out of power by 2019.

A wildcard province in all of this is North West, where the impact of the EFF was strongly felt in 2016, causing ANC support to plummet to 59.04 per cent. North West, Gauteng and the Western Cape house 42 per cent of the country's population. They hold the key to whether South Africa will be governed by a national coalition as early as 2019.

Simply put, the decline in ANC support in South Africa's vital metropolitan areas is accelerating rapidly, and seems set to continue into the 2020s. While the evidence is more equivocal at the provincial and national levels, the 2016 municipal elections clearly showed that growing numbers of ANC voters are willing to abstain or even change their votes in order to express their dissatisfaction with the governing party. Therefore, the ANC's slide seems set to continue in the 2019, 2021 and 2024 elections. If this happens at current rates, South Africa will soon be governed by a multitude of political coalitions at the municipal, provincial and national levels.

When the crew panics

But don't just take it from the data. In an extraordinary turn of events, some of the most vocal supporters of the theory that the ANC will soon lose its grip on political power are key role players within the ANC itself. Although some party bigwigs started whispering after the 2016 municipal polls that the ANC's majority could be in danger in 2019, it took Zuma's controversial cabinet reshuffle in March 2017 – widely interpreted as a move to consolidate the infamous Gupta family's hold over the country – to open the floodgates of panic in the party. Suddenly, a succession of senior party figures started talking about an imminent electoral disaster.

One of the first to sound the alarm was Pravin Gordhan. During a CNN interview conducted one month after his dismissal as finance minster which was broadcast worldwide, Gordhan stated: 'There are many of us who are extremely worried that if we continue as we are in the African National Congress, we are likely to lose the 2019 elections.'[11]

Soon afterwards, the ANC's Parliamentary chief whip, Jackson Mthembu, dramatically declared: 'We're not sure if we will continue to be free after 2019.'[12]

Former Mpumalanga premier Mathews Phosa also warned that the 'ANC will have to perform a miracle to obtain 50 per cent in 2019', while Gauteng ANC leader Paul Mashatile cautioned that 'muddling along as before might see us lose Gauteng in 2019', and that party leaders would 'only have themselves to blame' for such an outcome.

Other ANC leaders, including Zweli Mkhize and Lindiwe Sisulu, also warned starkly that the party's majority was in danger.[13]

But the most astonishing statement of all came from former president Kgalema Motlanthe. In April 2017, when asked in the course of a BBC interview whether he would vote for the ANC in 2019, he responded as follows: 'I don't know yet. It is not a given, because . . . we are forever snowed under in an avalanche of wrongdoing, and at some point there will be a tipping point.'[14]

If a former president's vote for the ANC can no longer be taken for granted, millions of others must also be having second thoughts.

Squandering dominance

Why, at this precise moment in our political history, is the ANC facing the prospect of losing its political dominance? While the rhetoric about the party's decline burst into the open following the 2016 municipal elections, and especially after the cabinet reshuffle in March 2017, the reasons for voter dissatisfaction with the ANC go back further.

In fact, the 2009 election result provided the first hint that the ANC was losing electoral momentum. As noted earlier, this was the first time that the party's support at the national level did not increase significantly compared to the preceding municipal election. Take a close look at Figure 3 (page 37) between 1994 and 2006, you can see a clear see-saw pattern. It shows that the ANC consistently received 8–10 per cent more votes during national elections compared to the preceding municipal elections.

Now look at the trend between 2006 and 2016. The see-saw is gone, replaced by a steady downward curve. The pattern was broken with the election of Zuma in 2009 when, for the first time, the ANC barely managed to increase its national vote compared to the previous municipal election, and this new trend accelerated in 2014. It is this trend that should worry party leaders most, because it suggests that the ANC vote in 2019 will drop *below* the historic low of 54.49 per cent that the party got in the 2016 municipal election.

Knowing that the 2009 campaign represented a turning point, we can begin to look at some of the reasons for the party's decline. Let's be guided by the opinion of South Africans themselves: in every Afrobarometer survey between 1999 and 2015, citizens have consistently said they are most concerned about three issues: corruption, unemployment and poverty, and crime. Above, all, the ANC's declining fortune since 2009 is rooted in its deteriorating performance in respect of these three metrics.

Most visible of these is undoubtedly the scourge of corruption, which has long plagued the ANC. Some of the earliest scandals date back to the presidency of Nelson Mandela; the first high-profile corruption case, known as the Sarafina scandal, surfaced less than two years after the ANC came to power. In 1996, then health minister Nkosazana Dlamini-Zuma (who lost to Ramaphosa in the ANC's 2017 leadership race), gave a close friend a R14 million tender to produce a theatre performance about the dangers of AIDS. In the months that followed, the ANC repeatedly chose to protect Dlamini-Zuma after she was caught lying to Parliament, and even after the funder of the production, the European Union, revealed that it had not approved the contract. As the *New York Times* reported: '. . . after more than two years in office, the ANC is developing a poor record on handling charges of corruption and misconduct within its ranks'.[15]

ANC leaders with a penchant for dodgy deals and access to the national piggy bank then kicked it up a notch with what became known as the ANC's 'original sin': the notorious arms deal. In early 1999, the ANC-led government rushed through a deal to purchase military equipment from a range of global suppliers. Despite the fact that the country had opted for social development over armed conflict just five years previously, the government insisted on buying new fighter jets, submarines, warships and military helicopters costing more than R90 billion (in 2017 rands).

International investigators from Britain, Germany, Sweden and France soon implicated ANC heavyweights, including Thabo Mbeki, Jacob Zuma, Tony Yengeni, Fana Hlongwana, Chippy Shaik and Jacob Zuma's financial adviser, Schabir Shaik, in bribery by arms suppliers totalling more than R1 billion.[16] Only Yengeni and Schabir Shaik were held even partly accountable: Yengeni served a mere four months in prison for receiving a luxury vehicle from one of the contractors, and Shaik was released on medical parole after serving only two years and four months of a 15-year sentence for one charge of fraud and two of corruption. The first corruption charge related to payments by Shaik to Zuma in order to further what the state described as a 'general corrupt relationship'. The second involved payments to Zuma by a French arms company, which Shaik had solicited. At the time of Shaik's release in 2009, the state alleged that he was 'terminally ill'. By 2017, however, he was still working at improving his golf handicap on some of South Africa's smoothest fairways.

The farcical pretend-investigations into the arms deal, including the findings in 2015 that there had been no wrongdoing[17] by a commission of inquiry set up by President Jacob Zuma, opened the gates to a flood of corruption surrounding the government and parastatals such as Eskom and Transnet that would eventually threaten to consume the ANC.

The year 2005 brought the 'Travelgate' scandal in which 40

MPs – 10 per cent of MPs in the National Assembly – were charged with benefiting from false travel claims to the value of R18 million. All 14 MPs who were eventually convicted were members of the ANC.

Two years later, in 2007, national police commissioner Jackie Selebi was charged with corruption, fraud, racketeering, and defeating the ends of justice for accepting bribes from drug dealers totalling more than R1.2 million. Soon after Selebi was fired (after spending months on suspension with full pay), his successor, Bheki Cele, irregularly awarded an inflated R500 million lease for South African Police Service headquarters in Pretoria and Durban to a billionaire businessman, Roux Shabangu.

Zuma's name had repeatedly cropped up during the fraud and corruption trial of his financial adviser, Schabir Shaik. In his judgement on 2 June 2005, Judge Hilary Squires referred to a 'mutually beneficial symbiosis' between Zuma and his adviser. On 14 June, President Thabo Mbeki dismissed Zuma as deputy president, pending an investigation into corruption charges. In December 2005, Zuma was also charged with raping the daughter of a close friend (he was eventually acquitted). In December 2007, after numerous delays engineered by Zuma (a strategy he would continue to use to good effect after becoming president), he was finally charged with 783 counts of corruption, money laundering, racketeering and fraud.

Amid a series of lengthy back-and-forths in court between Zuma and state prosecutors, the ANC held its 52nd national conference in Polokwane in December 2007. Despite the controversies swirling around Zuma, party members still thought it wise to elect him as party president, and a coterie of his most ardent supporters to other top positions. This led to the recall of Mbeki as South African president in September 2008, with Kgalema Motlanthe replacing him as placeholder president until the 2009 general elections, when Zuma would ascend to the national presidency.

In early 2009, the National Prosecuting Authority (NPA) removed the final obstacle on Zuma's path to the presidency when it dropped all 783 counts against him. The decision was taken after prosecutors had obtained a set of 'spy tapes' that allegedly contained evidence of a political conspiracy against Zuma.[18] The decision to drop the charges was taken despite the fact that no judge or anyone outside the top echelons of the prosecuting authority had ever listened to the tape recordings. Soon after, on 9 May 2009, Zuma was sworn in as president.

The ascent to power of a deeply compromised group of leaders turned the stream of corruption into a torrent. The seemingly endless list of politicians and officials who took to plundering state resources include several of Zuma's own ministers.

In early December 2013, the then Public Protector, Thuli Madonsela, found that communications minister Dina Pule had 'persistently lied' and conducted herself 'unethically' after she had used state funds to give her boyfriend a R6 million government tender. In the same week, Madonsela also found Zuma's then agriculture minister, Tina Joemat-Pettersson, guilty of maladministration as well as improper and unethical conduct in the irregular awarding of a R800 million fisheries tender.

Another star in this firmament is the minister of social development, Bathabile Dlamini. She grew up in Nkandla, seat of Jacob Zuma's infamous private compound in rural KwaZulu-Natal. She later helped to build the ANC Women's League (ANCWL) in that province. In 2006, Dlamini was one of 14 ANC MPs convicted of fraud in the 'Travelgate' scandal, and lost her position as an MP. However, at the 52nd National Conference of the ANC in December 2007, she was elected to the ANC's national executive committee and national working committee, allegedly because she campaigned for Zuma's election as ANC president. She was appointed as deputy minister of social development in May 2009, as minister of social development in November 2010, and became president of the ANCWL in 2015.

In 2017, Dlamini brought the country's welfare system to the brink of collapse when she failed to put in place a plan to pay social grants after a corrupt R10 billion contract with a private company had been nullified by the Constitutional Court. Instead, Dlamini obfuscated, and forced the court to extend the corrupt contract for another year.

In March 2017, Cosatu called on her to resign, failing which it would mobilise a 'massive countrywide worker protest' aimed at forcing her to vacate her position.[19] Later the same week, Corruption Watch joined a growing list of organisations and individuals calling for her dismissal. Despite this, Dlamini remained in Zuma's cabinet, allegedly because she supported Zuma's ex-wife, Nkosazana Dlamini-Zuma, in her bid for the ANC and eventually the national presidency. Indeed, in November 2017, Dlamini announced that the ANCWL had 'nominated' Dlamini-Zuma as its preferred candidate for the ANC presidency.

The list goes on. Land reform minister Gugile Nkwinti was accused of handing a R97 million farm meant for land redistribution to a friend; Pule's successor as communications minister,

Faith Muthambi, lied to the SABC board about the appointment of the deranged Hlaudi Motsoeneng (a Zuma pick) to head the public broadcaster; mining minister Mosebenzi Zwane allegedly flew to Switzerland to facilitate a mining deal on behalf of the Gupta family; and small business minister Lindiwe Zulu was linked to a R631 million tender that was improperly awarded for the construction of toilets in the Amathole district municipality in the Eastern Cape.

Then there were the scandals surrounding Jacob Zuma himself. They include the aforementioned 783 corruption counts, which still need to be thoroughly investigated. There is also the Nkandla fiasco, with the Constitutional Court ruling in 2016 that Zuma had violated his oath of office when he defied an order from the Public Protector to pay back a portion of the R246 million in public funds spent in upgrading his private palace at Nkandla in impoverished rural KwaZulu-Natal. Although Public Protector Thuli Madonsela only ruled that Zuma should pay back a relatively small portion of the total costs, her report on Nkandla revealed a disturbing string of irregularities.

Zuma also treated one of South Africa's most sensitive military installations, Waterkloof Air Force Base in Pretoria, as his personal taxi rank when he allegedly arranged clearance for his partners in crime, the Guptas, to land a passenger jet at the base. Police then escorted the Guptas and hundreds of guests to a family wedding at Sun City.

In mid-2017, a trove of leaked emails from the heart of the Gupta empire added fuel to the fire. During months of exposés in the media, the emails provided evidence of the 'shadow state' that Zuma and his wealthy benefactors had constructed since his ascent to power. Some of the more startling emails revealed how the Guptas had helped the Zuma family to obtain residency and multi-million-rand properties in the United Arab Emirates.[20] The cache also revealed how their relationship with Zuma helped the Guptas to seize informal control of state-owned enterprises like Eskom and Transnet.[21]

Zuma's anointment as party leader at Polokwane and the growing trail of scandals in the wake of this decision is the logical culmination of the corruption cancer that had metastasised and grown in the party ever since it came to power in 1994. Zuma and his patronage network did not create the culture of corruption in the ANC – but they perfected it and made it their own after Zuma became president in 2009.

Although the most visible, corruption is not the only long-term cause of the ANC's decline. Despite laudable efforts in the 1990s to help South Africa escape a debt trap, and further halting progress in the early 2000s, the ANC has also recently presided over an economic implosion. Economic underperformance, particularly since 2009, has led to a steady increase in poverty and unemployment, consistently identified in Afrobarometer surveys as the single most important issue facing South African society.

Between 1994 and 2006, the economy grew at an average of 3.5 per cent a year. Since then, the annual average has dropped to less than 2 per cent, falling to 0.3 per cent in 2016. And in late 2016 and early 2017, the ANC plunged South Africa into its second recession in a decade when GDP growth declined during two successive quarters. Since the country's population is increasing by 1.5 per cent a year, the simple reality of this economic collapse is that, during the past decade, South Africans have rapidly become poorer.

The ANC government's destruction of the economy is reflected in the unemployment rate. After slowly falling during the early years of democracy, in the decade since 2008, the percentage of people without work has rapidly increased (Figure 4), reaching its highest level in 14 years in 2017. Even in terms of a narrow definition of unemployment, which excludes people who have given up on trying to find work, almost three in every ten adults of working age could not find a job. In 2017, more than half of South Africans were living below the poverty line, on an income of R779 or less a month.[22]

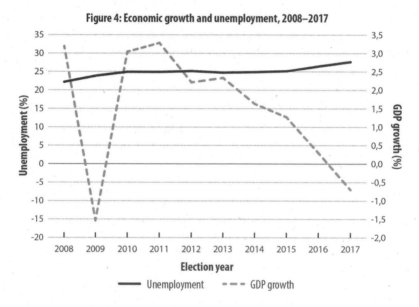

Figure 4: Economic growth and unemployment, 2008–2017

Source: Statistics South Africa.

In early 2017, poor economic growth, uncertainty about the ANC's economic policies, and fears about escalating corruption prompted the international credit ratings agencies Fitch as well as Standard & Poor's to cut the country's rand-denominated sovereign debt rating to sub-investment grade – commonly known as junk status. For the first time since the turn of the century, South Africa was no longer regarded as a safe destination for international investors.

The ratings downgrade is one of the key reasons why the ANC will probably not be able to reverse its decline in coming years. According to Afrobarometer's latest round of surveys, two thirds of South Africans already believe the government is managing the economy 'very badly', or 'fairly badly'.[23] If the ANC wanted to reverse its current downward trajectory, changing voters' overwhelmingly negative sentiment around the economy should be at the top of its to-do list.

But Zuma's 2017 cabinet reshuffle that triggered the downgrades effectively tied a ball and chain around the party's ankles. Junk status means that it will be much more expensive for the government to borrow money, significantly reducing the funds available to spend on poverty alleviation and on kick-starting economic growth. Even if it wanted to, the downgrades mean that it is now almost impossible for the ANC to fix the South African economy any time soon. It takes an average of seven years for a country to recover from junk status.[24] With negativity around the economy already at historic highs, and with the government unable to raise the money necessary to fund any kind of recovery, the ANC will probably lose power long before South Africa eventually recovers from junk status.

The ANC's performance on the third key metric identified by South Africans – crime – reflects a similar pattern. On the whole, crime rates first declined slowly but surely after the ANC took power. This was also true for some of the crimes most feared by South Africans, including murder, housebreaking and car-jacking. However, this trend reversed about a decade ago. Today, the number of murders, housebreakings and car hijackings per 100 000 people are far higher than they were ten years ago.

Given that the ANC inherited a country that already had one of the highest rates of violent crime in the world, it was perhaps understandable that voters were initially patient. Nobody could have turned the country into a peaceful paradise overnight. But citizens did want to see a gradual decrease in crime. Between 1994 and 2006, this was largely true, and the ANC could claim that it was making progress. However, as in the case of corruption and economic growth, the government has rapidly lost ground in the battle against crime during the past decade.

One of the key reasons for worsening personal safety in recent years is the chronic instability of corporate governance of the state's police and prosecuting services. As the Zuma cabal sought to avoid prosecution, crippling the investigative and prosecutorial independence of law enforcement agencies was one of its key survival strategies. As a result, South Africa has had no less than five police chiefs since Zuma became president, four of whom were eventually involved in corruption scandals themselves. The Hawks, supposedly South Africa's equivalent of the American FBI, also remains in a state of chaos, with an acting head in place since a Constitutional Court ruling that Zuma's appointment of the totally unqualified Berning Ntlemeza was irregular. Then there is the NPA head and Zuma sycophant Shaun Abrahams, who, in 2016, was embarrassingly forced to climb down from a political witch hunt against former finance minister Pravin Gordhan, and who failed to prosecute any members of the Zuma-Gupta cabal after hundreds of thousands of leaked emails exposed their brazen corruption.

The logical consequence of this maladministration is that the security services have lost what little ability they had to protect South Africans. For example, since 2011, the number of roadblocks organised by the police have declined by 74 per cent.[25] In 2016, the police were only able to identify suspects in a quarter of all murder cases, and in 18 per cent of robbery cases.[26] The implication is staggering: three out of every four people who committed a murder in 2016 have never been identified. The number of convictions obtained by the supposedly elite investigation unit, the Hawks, has also dropped by 83 per cent since 2011.[27] In short, the country's security services have been gutted.

For many South Africans, this is a matter of life and death. The murder rate has spiked by 20 per cent over the past five years. In the same period, cases of aggravated robbery have increased by 31.5 per cent (Figure 5). Statistics South Africa's 2016 Victims of Crime survey put it bluntly: 'South Africans feel that violent and property crime is increasing to the extent that the majority of households don't feel safe to walk alone in parks or allow their children to play freely in their neighbourhoods.'[28]

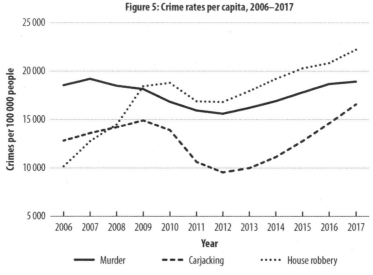

Figure 5: Crime rates per capita, 2006–2017

Source: Crime Stats SA.

By 2009 – precisely because it had made some progress in raising living standards during its first 15 years in power – the ANC faced a population with much higher expectations than the society it had inherited in 1994. In fact, the combination of social grants – which sustain 17 million people every month – with increased public sector employment meant that the ANC had succeeded in making sure that more than half of South Africa's 8.3 million middle-class citizens were black. But the middle-class black South Africans of 2009 had much higher expectations than the impoverished people of 1994 who had just emerged from the apartheid era. While the poorest people worry most about finding their next meal, middle-class citizens tend to care more about fighting crime and corruption, and finding good schools for their children.

Fatally for the ANC, just as the party faced an increasingly modern, wealthy and mobile society with higher expectations for the future, ANC members essentially surrendered any hope they had of meeting these expectations when they elected Zuma as leader. A decade into the 21st century, the ANC chose a semi-literate man mired in allegations of corruption to lead a modern market economy deeply integrated into the global system. The ANC drank poison when it chose Zuma at its Polokwane conference.

But it was a slow poison. As a result, the country's backsliding over the last decade in terms of mounting corruption, economic decline, and rampant crime is not enough to explain why the ANC is only now in danger of losing its hegemony. Even though the 2009 and 2014 election results showed that the party was slipping, Zuma's government was still returned to power with an impressive 62.15 per cent in 2014. Why should 2019 be any different? The answer to this question is all about timing and semantics.

Political crises are never triggered solely by failures of governance. Instead, longer-term trends need to coalesce around a visible focal point that encapsulates the broader crisis in the public mind. This is the reason why phrases like 'the assassination in Sarajevo', 'Watergate', and 'the Rubicon speech' became short-hand references to the crisis that triggered the First World War, the corruption of Richard Nixon, and the death throes of PW Botha's presidency.

On 31 March 2016, the Constitutional Court provided the spark that ignited the powder keg of simmering resentment and unmet expectations when it ruled that Zuma had violated the Constitution when he failed to comply with a report by the Public Protector to pay back a portion of the public funds spent on his private home. Like Sarajevo, Watergate, and Rubicon, the ANC's impending disaster now had a name: Nkandla.

The Nkandla scandal, involving state expenditure of R246 million to upgrade Zuma's private compound, quickly became a byword for all that had gone wrong in the previous decade. It illustrated how brazen the new elite had become in stealing from South African citizens. Built on a hill, and surrounded by a sea of poverty, Nkandla also showed vividly how the majority of South Africans remained trapped in poverty while a small group of predators fed off their misery. The scandal even highlighted the collapse of the security services, as Zuma roped in then police minister Nathi Nhleko as his primary defender. During Parliamentary meetings and media conferences, Nhleko sweated profusely as he claimed that an amphitheatre was actually a break wall, and that a swimming pool was a 'fire pool' meant to supply fire fighters with water.

Unlike any previous event in modern South Africa, the Nkandla ruling squarely focused the public mind on the ANC's failings. Ignited by the scandal, the suffering induced by years of corruption, economic decline and crime finally started showing its face at the polling booth, five months after the Constitutional Court ruling. But the 2016 municipal elections were just the beginning. As if the Nkandla scandal wasn't bad enough, Zuma's corruption again focused the public mind on the ANC's failings when, from late 2016 onwards, the term 'state capture' was introduced into the public lexicon. This time, the damage went much further than just Zuma.

The release of Public Protector Thuli Madonsela's *State of Capture* report in November 2016, and the stream of exposés in the media following the massive Gupta email leak, implicated more than half of the ANC's cabinet ministers in a systematic attempt to plunder state resources in South Africa's new order. This includes everyone from President Jacob Zuma and finance minister Malusi Gigaba, public service minister Faith Muthambi and co-operative governance minister Des van Rooyen, communications minister Ayanda Dlodlo, and Eskom CEOs Brian Molefe and Matshela Koko to ANC Youth League president Collen Maine. To top it all, the Gupta emails revealed how the family had drafted ANC media statements and enlisted the help of the UK public relations firm Bell Pottinger to prop up their predatory conduct.

Built on the foundation of a failing economy, endemic corruption, and increasing violence, the Nkandla and state capture scandals are the trigger moments that have caused the ANC ship to start sinking. Even with hundreds of thousands of leaked emails, we almost certainly haven't seen the full extent of the state capture scandal yet, and the bad news is likely to keep coming in the lead-up to 2019. In the meantime, we have at least one piece of evidence that shows just how bad the damage to the ANC could be.

The first full municipal by-election since the state capture scandal broke took place on 29 November 2017 in the Metsimaholo local municipality in the northern Free State. The 2016 election had already produced a hung council, with an ANC-led alliance and a DA-led alliance holding 21 seats each. When the council deadlocked, and failed to pass a budget, the national government disbanded it and called for new elections.

In 2016, the ANC had received only 45 per cent of the vote in the municipality, down from 62 per cent in 2011. But things went from bad to worse in the November 2017 by-election when the SACP decided to contest the by-election on its own. In the wake of the ANC's latest scandals, the SACP got 8.7 per cent, while support for the ANC imploded, with the party garnering only 34.6 per cent in what was once a municipal stronghold. The collapse was particularly pronounced in the townships, where support for the ANC plummeted from 82 per cent in 2011 to only 45 per cent in 2017.

Given that Metsimaholo is demographically similar to large parts of Gauteng, the by-election result should set alarm bells ringing in Luthuli House, the ANC's head office. Following the ANC's slide in 2016, Metsimaholo confirmed that the party was on a one-way path to losing power.

It occurs slowly, then all at once

While it may seem as if the ANC has suddenly lost its dominant grip on political power, its decline has been a long time coming. At the most basic level, the party operates within an electoral system actively geared towards promoting coalitions and making it difficult for any one party to become dominant. It was always unrealistic to imagine that the ANC could swim forever against the tide.

But the ANC has also not done itself any favours on other levels during the past decade. It has driven the national economy to the edge of an abyss, inflicting growing hardships on many citizens. It has also looked on as South Africa has become an ever more violent society, with daily news of brutal crimes. Most visibly, amidst the suffering of most of its citizens, the party has allowed corruption to become endemic. Like a perverse version of King Midas, the ANC has reached a point where everything it touches becomes infected with corruption.

But it took the outrageous Nkandla and state capture scandals to finally galvanise our deeply divided society into action. Voters took the previously unprecedented step of punishing the ANC during the 2016 elections, and thousands of protestors flooded the streets in the wake of the Gupta cabinet reshuffle. Whatever remedial steps the ANC may aim to take in the run-up to 2019 are unlikely to overcome the depth of voters' disillusionment, which has built up slowly but surely during the past decade.

South Africa has entered a phase of rapid change that will soon see blind loyalty to the ANC replaced by a fractured political landscape dominated by coalitions. It is already far too late for the party to self-correct in the hopes of hanging on to its dominant position. Instead, the ANC will soon find that it has tried to close the stable door after the horse had bolted.

Chapter Three

A fragmented opposition

While the ANC is rapidly losing its grip on power, there's a potential complicating factor standing in the way of coalitions becoming the new normal. As the ANC has so powerfully demonstrated, it is certainly possible for one party to attain a dominant position in our political system if a large majority of voters prefer this. Once support for the ANC drops below 50 per cent, won't another party simply take its place as a hegemonic force that controls the national government and more than half of all municipalities and provinces? The short answer is no. The ANC's electoral decline is unlikely to benefit any single opposition party to the extent that it will become a dominant electoral force. The key consideration in this regard is whether the voters who are abandoning the ANC are likely to vote for one other party, or whether multiple opposition parties stand to benefit from the ANC's decline.

A long walk to power

Let's start by looking at the potential for South Africa's official opposition, the DA, to replace the ANC as the dominant force in South African politics. In contrast to the ANC, the DA has traditionally done best in municipal rather than national elections. In particular, the party has grown consistently in metropolitan municipalities since 2006. It now dominates politics in Cape Town, and governs Nelson Mandela Bay, Tshwane, and Johannesburg as the senior partner in formal coalition and minority governments. Figure 6 displays the DA's electoral performance in metro elections from 2000 to 2016, and projects this up to 2021.

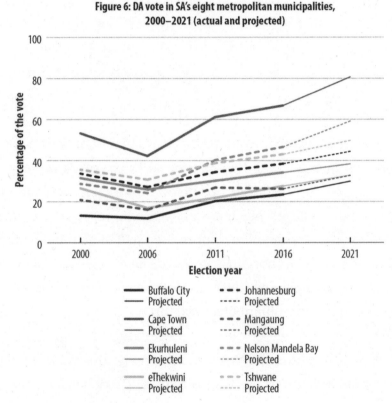

Figure 6: DA vote in SA's eight metropolitan municipalities, 2000–2021 (actual and projected)

Source: Electoral Commission of South Africa.

The results are highly significant. In the first place, the DA looks set to maintain its majority in Cape Town well into the future. It is also trending upwards in all seven other metros. However, it is only in Nelson Mandela Bay and Tshwane (and perhaps eventually Johannesburg) where it has a realistic chance of achieving an outright majority (more than 50 per cent of all votes) within the next decade. It is unlikely to capture Buffalo City (East London and Bisho), eThekwini (Durban), Mangaung (Bloemfontein) and Ekurhuleni (East Rand) on its own any time soon.

With at least half of the country's eight biggest cities still out of the DA's reach, what about other municipalities and provincial governments? The Western Cape is an interesting case, providing the single strongest argument in support of the idea that the DA may soon take over more of the country's provinces and municipalities, both urban and rural. Remarkably, the DA's current dominance in the Western Cape is akin to the ANC's overwhelming support in most parts of the country during the early 2000s, when it was just about the only game in town. In the Western Cape, the DA has now become the only game in town.

But this wasn't always the case. As recently as 2006, the DA had majorities in only two Western Cape municipalities. The ANC controlled three outright, and had more support than the DA in 17 more. But 2006 was also the year in which the DA was able to cobble together a seven-party coalition which took control of Cape Town, the province's political crown jewel (Chapter Nine returns to the remarkable story of the 2006 Cape Town coalition).

The multiparty alliance elected the DA's Helen Zille as mayor of Cape Town. Between 2006 and 2011, her administration managed to turn the failing municipality around in financial and administrative terms. By the time the 2011 local elections came around, the National Treasury and external credit ratings agencies were regularly rating Cape Town as the best-run metro in the country, and the city consistently achieved unqualified audit opinions, attesting to its sound financial management.[1]

Cape Town's success provided a political springboard for the DA to expand into the rest of the Western Cape, and Zille's party masterfully took advantage of the opportunity. During the 2009 provincial elections, the DA built its campaign around its growing track record of clean governance in Cape Town. The strategy paid off, and the party wrested control of the provincial government from the ANC.

In the 2011 municipal polls, the party kicked its campaigning up another notch by adopting the slogan 'We Deliver For All'. It again vigorously canvassed voters in the Western Cape on the basis that it was no longer just an opposition party; instead, the Cape Town experience had turned it into a party of government, and one that governed well. The message stuck. Building on its 2009 provincial victory, the DA completely flipped the script in the province's 30 municipalities, winning 12 outright, while the ANC did not gain a majority in a single municipality. The rout continued in 2016, when the DA won 17 municipalities outright. The ANC again failed to get a single outright majority.

The Western Cape experience shows that, at the municipal and provincial levels at least, voters who abandon the ANC may indeed vote en masse for a single opposition party. After 2006, Western Cape voters who were dissatisfied with ANC maladministration did not split evenly into different groups supporting the ACDP (which held the position of deputy mayor in Cape Town), the FF+, COPE, the UDM, the Africa Muslim Party, the Universal Party, and the DA, even though these parties were all part of the Cape Town coalition. Instead, the DA was able to take control of the Cape Town narrative and convince voters that it was the real reason for the city's turnaround. Its glossy 2011 election manifesto was even entitled *The Cape Town Story*.[2] As a result, a large majority of voters rewarded the DA, but none of its six original coalition partners.

In essence, the DA's strategy in the Western Cape was first to wrest control of the metro away from the ANC through a coalition; turn Cape Town into a well-run municipality; take credit for the improvement; and then carry that message into the province's rural hinterland. Tracking the party's growth between 2006 and 2016 shows a striking pattern: the DA first took over areas closer to Cape Town, while its influence weakened further from the metro. By 2016, this incremental process meant that almost every municipality within about 450 kilometres of Cape Town was under DA control. Beyond 450 kilometres, the ANC remained in charge (although its majorities were shrinking).

The spread of DA power from the metropolis to the surrounding rural areas probably had a lot to do with information flows. People who lived closer to the city visited Cape Town more regularly, and knew more people who lived there. These visitors took the DA's story of progress back to their own communities. But it naturally took longer for the DA's Cape Town message to reach those people who lived further away, knew fewer people in the city, and visited less regularly. The message was widely spread in municipalities close to the city, but thinned out further from Cape Town.

From a national perspective, this paints a promising picture for the DA. Just as in Cape Town in 2006, the party took over mayoral positions in Nelson Mandela Bay, Tshwane, and Johannesburg after the 2016 elections by cobbling together multiparty working arrangements. In the hopes of replicating its Western Cape experience, the first step would be for the DA to clean up the administration of these three metros – no small task after decades of ANC misrule.[3]

If it does succeed in turning these metros around, the party could build its 2019 provincial and 2021 municipal campaigns around these success stories. Based on the Western Cape template, the DA's aim would be to take over dozens of municipalities and eventually win provincial office in Gauteng, the Northern Cape, and possibly the Eastern Cape. It is probably the best strategy the DA could follow, and it will be fascinating to watch this dynamic unfold.

However, it is doubtful whether the party will be able to replicate the Western Cape pattern in most other parts of the country. Western Cape politics have always differed from those in the rest of the country. In 1994, the NP won the Western Cape even as the rest of the country (except for KwaZulu-Natal) supported the ANC. Although the ANC eventually merged with a faction of the NP to gain control of the province, it was never as popular there as it was in most parts of the country. The Western Cape was never fully under the ANC's spell.

The reasons for this have to do with economics and demographics. Even before the DA took over, the Western Cape was the second wealthiest province in South Africa (after Gauteng) in terms of GDP per capita, and had the lowest unemployment rate of all nine provinces.[4] The province has excellent transport and communication infrastructure, and features the highest literacy and school completion rates in the country.[5] Overall, then, residents of the Western Cape are wealthier, more educated, and have access to better infrastructure than most other South Africans.

The province's demographics are also different from most of the country (although some parts of the Eastern and Northern Cape have similar demographic profiles). It is the only province where black people are not a demographic majority. Coloured people constitute nearly half of the population, while the province is also home to a higher proportion of white South Africans relative to other regions. Afrikaans is the primary language for half of the Western Cape's population, as opposed to only 13.5 per cent of the national population.[6]

The profile of DA supporters largely reflects the economic and demographic composition of its Western Cape support base. The latest available public opinion poll on the profiles of political party support was conducted by Ipsos in late 2013. While those results are outdated, they provide some interesting insights. The results show that, on average, DA voters were better educated and wealthier than ANC (or EFF) voters. About half of DA voters were white, 27 per cent coloured, and 20 per cent black.[7] Afrikaans-speakers made up about half of all DA supporters, and English-speakers about 32 per cent.[8]

While it is thus safe to say that the party's message has resonated with wealthier minority voters to a far greater extent than those of any other party – it has indeed turned the DA into the most ethnically diverse political party in South African history – the big question is whether the DA's strategy of using the Nelson Mandela Bay/Tshwane/Johannesburg story to win over voters in the rural Eastern Cape as well as in the rural areas of Limpopo, North West, the Free State and Mpumalanga which surround metropolitan Gauteng, could succeed. This strategy worked well in the relatively wealthy, mostly Afrikaans- and English-speaking minority communities of the Western Cape. But it is still unclear whether it will work in regions where most voters are black, don't speak Afrikaans or English, and are much poorer.

Nevertheless, the 2016 elections showed that the DA has a much higher electoral ceiling than most people thought possible a decade previously. If it can govern the big cities successfully during the next few years, it may soon be in outright control of Cape Town, Nelson Mandela Bay, Tshwane, and Johannesburg. Given the ANC's implosion in the metros, the DA could soon also be the senior partner in a coalition government in Ekurhuleni (which would give the party control over all of Gauteng's major municipalities), while trending upwards in Buffalo City, eThekwini and Mangaung. Rural regions most likely to swing eventually to the DA are located in the western parts of the Northern and Eastern Cape, home to some minority groups that still support the ANC. Proof of this is the fact that the DA has also grown significantly in many smaller regional centres such as Kimberley, Springbok, and Cradock.

The best-case scenario for the DA during the next decade is to retain its majorities in Cape Town and the Western Cape, win control of Gauteng's municipalities as well as its provincial government, win Nelson Mandela Bay outright, and win provincial elections in the Northern Cape and Eastern Cape. If this does materialise, it would constitute a political achievement that was unthinkable even two elections ago. But even then, DA majorities in much of the central and eastern parts of the country – including Limpopo, Mpumalanga, KwaZulu-Natal, North West, and the Free State – would remain highly unlikely.

While the DA's best-case scenario is not impossible, economic and demographic realities mean that its future gains in Gauteng as well as in the Northern and Eastern Cape will probably result from its participation in coalitions. A more realistic future for the DA is probably one in which the party remains dominant in the Western Cape, and heads coalition governments (at the municipal and provincial levels) in Gauteng, the Northern Cape, and parts of the Eastern Cape. Despite the DA's impressive recent gains, it remains highly unlikely that it will gain outright control of more than half of South Africa's municipalities and provinces within the next decade. In turn, this means the party is unlikely to get more than 50 per cent of the national vote in the near future.

Rise of the spoilers

A compounding challenge facing the DA's attempts to gain majority support among poorer black communities in the central and eastern parts of the country is the emergence of the EFF as a spoiler or kingmaker in some significant municipalities. Although the EFF gained only 8.24 per cent of the national vote in the 2016 municipal elections, and did not win a majority in even one municipality, it probably played a decisive role in dragging the ANC below 50 per cent *and* preventing the DA from gaining outright majorities in some key places.

For example, in Nelson Mandela Bay, the DA ended up with 46.66 per cent, the ANC with 41.50 per cent, and the EFF with 5.03 per cent. In Tshwane, the DA got 43.10 per cent, the ANC 41.48 per cent, and the EFF 11.64 per cent. In both of these cases, it is easy to see how the EFF played an important role in keeping both the ANC and DA below the 50 per cent threshold. Aside from its impact on the metro results, the EFF also made significant gains in parts of the North West and Limpopo.

In Rustenburg, it dragged down the ANC's share of the vote from 73.82 per cent in 2011 to a mere 48.27 per cent in 2016, and the DA's from 20.29 per cent to 15.90 per cent, while the EFF itself won 26.44 per cent of the vote during its first election in Rustenburg. It had a similar impact in Polokwane – Julius Malema's home town – where the ANC's share of the vote dropped precipitously from 80.24 per cent to 57.20 per cent, and the DA's from 11.43 per cent to 10.91 per cent, with the EFF taking 28.33 per cent.

But despite its relatively rapid rise in some isolated regions as well as its high national Parliamentary and media profile, 91 out of every 100 South Africans have never voted for the EFF, and the party has never attempted to govern even one municipality, let alone a province. In terms of hard numbers, and in the bigger scheme of the country's politics, the EFF remains a fringe player that has a long way to go to gain anything approaching a dominant position at any level of government.

The final opposition parties to consider are the IFP and its breakaway, the National Freedom Party (NFP). It may be difficult to recall today, but during the 1990s, the IFP posed one of the greatest potential threats to ANC hegemony. The party dominated local and provincial politics in KwaZulu-Natal, and as a Zulu ethnic-based formation, it theoretically had the potential to cause a split within the ANC along ethnic lines. At more than 20 per cent of the population, Zulus constitute the single largest ethnic bloc in South Africa. If the IFP had managed to unite all Zulu voters under its flag, it could have seriously damaged the ANC's standing as a dominant force among black voters.

That did not happen. Instead, the ANC slowly ate into the IFP's support in KwaZulu-Natal, eventually winning outright control of the province in 2009. The IFP was further weakened when, in 2011, a faction of its leaders defected to form the ANC-aligned NFP. The newly formed party garnered more than 10 per cent of the votes in KwaZulu-Natal in the 2011 election, reducing the once provincially mighty IFP to only 15 per cent support in the province. The split in the IFP, coupled with its precipitous decline over the past two decades and its inability to break out of its ethnic enclave, means that both the IFP and the NFP have no chance of becoming a nationally dominant electoral force.

Figure 7 (overleaf) summarises the current state of play among opposition parties. With 27.02 per cent of the vote in 2016, the DA is clearly the best placed to challenge the ANC. But while the DA's recent growth has been impressive, it would need to almost double its current share of the vote to gain an outright national majority. The voting shares of all other opposition parties remain below 10 per cent, which means they have no realistic chance of becoming a dominant force in South African politics in the near future.

What about a party that doesn't yet exist, or has never fought an election? Given the growing tensions in the ANC alliance, one or more ANC splinter groups could contest the 2019 elections. This could include a workers' party established by SAFTU, the labour federation formed by former Cosatu secretary-general Zwelinzima Vavi. The SACP could also follow up its contestation of the Metsimaholo by-election in November 2017 by fielding its own candidates independently of the ANC in 2019. However, recent history tells us that any ANC splinter party would struggle

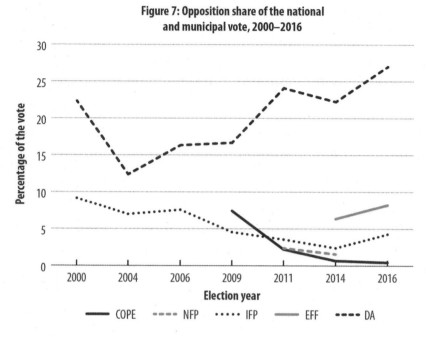

Figure 7: Opposition share of the national and municipal vote, 2000–2016

Source: Electoral Commission of South Africa.

to garner even 8 per cent of the national vote during its first few elections.

COPE was the first major group to defect from the ANC after Thabo Mbeki's recall. Founded in 2008, COPE won 7.42 per cent of the national vote in 2011. However, the party was soon crippled by leadership squabbles, and its support collapsed to 0.48 per cent in the 2016 elections. The second ANC splinter group, the EFF, won only 6.35 per cent of the vote in its first election in 2014, increasing to 8.31 per cent in 2016. Based on the experiences of COPE and the EFF, it is highly unlikely that new ANC spinoff parties would fare much better during the next decade.

However, as was made abundantly clear in the Metsimaholo by-election, more breakaways would further weaken the ANC.

70

With the party already in danger of losing the national government as well as the Western Cape, Gauteng and even North West
in 2019, the loss of another 8–10 per cent of support to splinter
groups would be catastrophic. While further splits in the ANC
are unlikely to suddenly produce a new dominant player, they are
sure to hasten the ANC's decline as the hegemonic party.

The reality is that South Africa's opposition party landscape is
highly fragmented. Over the first 20 years of democracy, an ever
shifting constellation of opposition groups have fought over the
scraps as the mighty ANC kept chugging along. But now that the
ANC is faltering, the fractured nature of opposition politics means
that no single group stands at the ready to replace the ANC as a
hegemonic force. If and when support for the ANC drops below
50 per cent, it will probably still be the biggest political grouping
in the country. But it will no longer be the first among equals.
Without an overwhelming majority that empowers the party to
ride roughshod over the coalition requirements of South Africa's
electoral framework, a humbled ANC will find itself in the same
position as all other parties: struggling to cobble together governing alliances. With no opposition party in a position to replace
the ANC as the first among equals, the coalition era will suddenly
be in full swing.

The end of forever

Two key ingredients are necessary to bake a coalition cake. First,
a country must have a set of electoral rules that encourage the
formation of coalition governments. Second, no single political
party should be able to consistently obtain electoral majorities
on its own. Instead, for coalitions to become the norm, political

power must be dispersed in relatively even proportion among different political parties. Since 1994, South Africa always had the first ingredient in its cupboard, but the ANC's electoral dominance meant that it lacked the second. Historian Hermann Giliomee's prediction in 1998 that 'The ANC [is] atop a dominant-party regime that figures to endure through the elections scheduled for 1999, 2004, and beyond'[9] has been proven correct.

But although Jacob Zuma may still think that the ANC will rule forever, 'forever' is fast coming to an end. The dominant-party regime is dying. The ANC's falling fortunes mean that, after 2019, political support will probably be divided much more evenly among South Africa's political parties. Once this second ingredient is in place, coalition governments will follow.

What remains to be seen is whether this coalition cake will actually be a good one. After all, there is more to becoming a successful baker than just mixing together different ingredients. Just as a good cake requires the baker to understand the thermodynamics of baking, so too do political leaders and citizens require a firm understanding of the dynamics inherent in coalition governments if they are to succeed.

From 2019 onwards, any government's efforts to improve the lives of ordinary South Africans will depend above all on their ability to build and manage successful coalitions.

Chapter Four

Designed for tomorrow

South Africa's adoption of an electoral system that encourages coalitions was partly based on optimism about the future. During the constitutional negotiations in the early 1990s, people from all walks of life gathered around the negotiating table in a sustained search for win-win solutions that would protect and promote the interests of all South Africans. The founders of the new order hoped that proportional representation would encourage political parties to form governing coalitions.

The architects of the new Constitution were influenced by the pioneering research of the Dutch political scientist Arend Lijphart, who argued that 'consociational' democracy – based on proportional representation and power-sharing – was more appropriate for ethnically divided societies than 'majoritarianism'. Lijphart's argument was intuitively appealing because South Africa was a deeply divided country haunted by the threat of a racial war. Therefore, many of the founders believed that political coalitions would be required to address the crises that were sure to arise out of the country's inherently polarised environment.[1]

Role players in the negotiated settlement sought to learn from the rest of the world. In a 1998 journal article, Lijphart noted that 'the South African case of consociationalism is unusual in that the negotiators were familiar with and influenced by the consociational model and various historical precedents of power-sharing'.[2] This again reinforces the fact that the country's adoption of a coalition-based system was no accident: it reflected the founders' deeply held belief that power-sharing among different political parties would lead to better outcomes than if one group continually dominated the others.

Lijphart defined consociationalism – or what might more elegantly and optimistically be called 'co-operative democracy' – in terms of four principles: (1) the government must be controlled by a 'broadly representative coalition of all significant groups'; (2) there must be a minimum level of territorial or non-territorial federalism and decentralisation; (3) the government system should be based on 'proportionality, especially with regard to political representation'; and (4) political minorities must have veto power 'concerning issues of vital and fundamental importance to minorities'.[3]

A glimpse of tomorrow

These conditions were briefly in place when a Government of National Unity (GNU) governed South Africa between April 1994 and June 1996.[4] In this period, which was primarily aimed at facilitating the drafting of a final Constitution, the ANC governed the country in coalition with the NP and the IFP. This was because the interim Constitution adopted in 1993 specified that any party with more than 5 per cent of the vote was entitled to be part of the cabinet, while any party with more than 20 per cent had the right to appoint one deputy president. In the event, three par ties qualified for inclusion in the GNU: the ANC, with 62.65 per cent of the vote in the 1994 elections; the NP, with 20.39 per cent; and the IFP, with 10.54 per cent.

During the first two years of Nelson Mandela's presidency, the country therefore had two deputy presidents: Thabo Mbeki from the ANC, and FW de Klerk from the NP. Based on a power-sharing formula spelled out in the interim Constitution, the three coalition partners also struck a deal that handed the ANC control over the powerful security and foreign affairs portfolios, as well as frontline service delivery portfolios such as education, health, public enterprises, public works, and housing. In exchange, the NP secured six ministerial portfolios: finance, constitutional development, agriculture, mining, welfare, and environmental affairs. Finally, IFP leader Mangosuthu Buthelezi became minister of home affairs, and his party also landed the correctional services and arts portfolios.[5]

Although the interim Constitution allowed for the GNU to remain in place until the 1999 election, the NP decided to end this arrangement in May 1996, just one week after the final Constitution was adopted by a resounding 86 per cent of Parliamentarians. In June, FW de Klerk resigned as second deputy president, and the six NP ministers were replaced by ANC appointees. The NP's decision to withdraw was based on a combination of factors, including the lack of a stronger power-sharing provision in the final Constitution, unhappiness about its perceived lack of influence in the government, and the need for the party to position itself as an opposition force in the lead-up to the 1999 election.[6]

The NP's withdrawal signified the end of the GNU. It was a disappointing conclusion to a coalition government that had achieved previously unthinkable successes. There is little doubt that the period between April 1994 and June 1996 was one of the most productive, co-operative and successful periods in South African political history. Working in unison, the coalition partners drove the process of finalising a progressive new Constitution founded on the values of equality and human rights, lauded by some international observers as 'the most admirable Constitution in the history of the world'.[7]

The GNU also stabilised the country after years of political, social and economic upheaval. Following nearly a decade of economic stagnation, growth quickly bounced back to 3.2 per cent in 1994, 3.1 per cent in 1995, and 4.3 per cent in 1996.[8] The GNU further co-ordinated the monumental task of integrating the fragmented legal structures and systems under apartheid – with different sets of laws for 11 different territories – into a single set of laws for the entire country.

Along the same lines, the GNU integrated 195 different government departments with 1.1 million staff members in various racially or ethnically defined public administrations into a single public service.[9] It introduced civilian oversight over the armed forces, and integrated 10 000 combatants from the ANC and other militias into the 95 000-strong South African Defence Force.[10] It also created nine new provinces, and successfully conducted the first ever democratic municipal elections in 1995.

Nicholas Haysom, who worked as Mandela's legal adviser during the GNU period and subsequently joined the United Nations as an adviser to conflict-ridden governments around the world on how to build successful power-sharing coalitions, later described the GNU's achievements as singular:

Within a matter of days, the government had to trans-form [the government] system . . . A large multinational corporation would probably have taken years to effect what we did within a matter of months. We redesigned the civil service, filled new leadership positions at three levels of government, defined responsibilities, and created brand new institutions like a Constitutional Court with the power to strike down legislation that was not in compliance with the new Bill of Rights.[11]

The GNU period gave South Africans a brief glimpse into the promise held by coalition governments in fractured societies like our own. Indeed, amid the crisis and destruction wrought by the Zuma administration, analysts have repeatedly suggested that the time has come for the country to create a new GNU as the only way to repair the damage.[12] The arguments in favour of a new GNU are precisely the same as those offered by Lijphart and supported by many of the Constitution writers in the 1990s: by giving multiple social groups a direct stake in government, a GNU encourages co-operation, compromise, and joint problem-solving, thereby reducing the likelihood of violent conflict or of one group exploiting another. With the ANC on track to get less than 50 per cent of the vote in the 2019 national and provincial elections, coalition 'governments of national unity' could soon become the new political normal.

Look to the world

The South African GNU is hardly the only example of an effective coalition government. Many countries have adopted coalition-based systems, and in some of these places, the compromise and co-operation inherent to governing through coalitions have helped power their societies to prosperity. In fact, of the top 10 countries on the UNDP's 2016 Human Development Index, all except one – Singapore – was governed by a coalition, as were 13 of the top 20.[13]

Over the past century, coalition governments have become the norm throughout Europe. In fact, between 1945 and 2014, only 12 per cent of all governments in Europe were *not* coalitions (this number includes countries like the United Kingdom and France, which have winner-take-all systems where the government is almost always controlled by only one party).[14] It would be no exaggeration to regard Europe as the Coalition Continent.

Perhaps the greatest example of how effective coalition governance can be in overcoming divisions and creating shared prosperity is Germany, which was tied for second place on the 2016 Human Development Index. When South Africa's constitutional framework was being developed, Germany was often explicitly cited as a model of how well political power-sharing can work.

During the Cold War from 1949 until 1989, Germany was divided into two countries. While East Germany became a stagnant Soviet proxy state mired in poverty, West Germany underwent a remarkable process of reconstruction, with support from the American Marshall Plan, which became known as the *Wirtschaftswunder* (economic miracle).

Germany had been devastated during the Second World War. Many cities had been turned into rubble, and 20 per cent of all houses in the country had been destroyed. Food production in 1947 was only half what it was in 1938, and rationing meant that people had to survive on a meagre 1 040 to 1 550 calories a day. Many men of working age had died in the war, and industrial output in 1947 was only one third of the 1938 level.[15]

By the 1960s, West Germany was nearly unrecognisable, following a spectacular economic recovery. This was rooted in the economic theory of Ordo-liberalism, and its ideas about creating a *Soziale Marktwirtschaft* (social market economy). However, as with most good economic ideas, it required a healthy dose of political will to succeed. Fortunately, West Germany was governed by a succession of ambitious coalition governments that included the main centre-right party as well as liberals between 1949 and 1966. Writing in 1955, Yale University economist Henry Wallich poignantly captured the essence of the transformation brought about by the West German coalitions: 'The spirit of the country changed overnight. The gray, hungry, dead-looking figures wandering about the streets in their everlasting search for food came to life.'[16]

As in most of the world, the political winds shifted in the late 1960s. From 1966 to 1969, West Germany featured its first grand coalition, with the two biggest political parties – the centre-right Christian Democrats and the centre-left Social Democrats – forming a governing alliance. From 1969 to 1982, West Germany was governed by a coalition of social democrats and liberals, before the centre-right/liberal coalition made a comeback in the early 1980s.

By the time that the Berlin Wall came down in 1989, West Germany had been transformed into an economic powerhouse. By contrast, authoritarian East Germany was still trapped in poverty. Following the collapse of the Soviet Union, communist East

Germany was incorporated into the prosperous and capitalist West Germany on 3 October 1990. After reconstructing a devastated economy in the West, the newly reunited German state faced its next daunting challenge: fixing the inequality that existed between the rich West and the poor East.

A series of coalition governments – now representing the entire territory of modern Germany and a population of 78 million people – took up the challenge. Under the chancellorship of Helmut Kohl, a coalition between the Christian Democrats and the liberals lasted from 1990 until 1998. This was followed by a prominent left turn when the Social Democrats and the Green Party governed together from 1998 until 2005. In 2005, Germany got its second grand coalition when the Christian Democrats led by Angela Merkel partnered with the Social Democrats. Merkel's party then briefly co-governed with the liberals between 2009 and 2013 before reconstituting the grand coalition with the Social Democrats in 2013.

By the mid-2010s, while inequalities still existed, successive German coalition governments had once again achieved improbable success. In 1990, East Germany's GDP per capita was only 30 per cent that of the West. Only 25 years after the fall of the Berlin Wall, GDP per capita in the former East Germany equalled 70 per cent of that in the former West. Life expectancy had also been equalised, while unemployment in the East was at its lowest level since 1990 (although still higher than in the West). In 2014, reflecting on the 25th anniversary of the fall of the Wall, Gert Wagner, an economist at the Berlin University of Technology, pointed out that 'There is no [other] example in history that an economy with such low productivity could catch up in 25 years to a really high, a really efficient and effective economy as we have in West Germany.'[17]

Outside of Europe, where almost all democracies are based around coalitions, India – the world's second biggest country, with 1.2 billion people – provides another intriguing, if more mixed, example. Following its independence from Great Britain on 15 August 1947, Indian politics was dominated by the Indian National Congress. Like the ANC in South Africa, the Indian National Congress was seen as the party of liberation, and enjoyed overwhelming electoral support during the first decades of democracy. Between 1951 and 1977, 'Congress' consistently controlled between 54 per cent and 75 per cent of the seats in the Lok Sabha (the Indian version of the National Assembly).[18]

However, in the early 1970s, Congress governments became increasingly authoritarian as well as increasingly corrupt. In a highly charged atmosphere marked by mounting political unrest, Prime Minister Indira Gandhi was found guilty of electoral fraud by the High Court in mid-1975. The court ruled that she had to give up her Parliamentary seat, and banned her from contesting any election for six years. In response, the government declared a national state of emergency that severely restricted civil liberties. Voters punished the Congress for the state of emergency at the 1977 polls. For the first time in post-independence India, Congress lost its majority as the opposition Janata alliance, an amalgamation of seven parties, swept to victory. In coalition with two other parties, the new government controlled two thirds of the seats in Parliament while Congress looked in from the cold.

While the Janata coalition ended the emergency and amended the Indian Constitution to make it more difficult for future governments to abuse a state of emergency, the alliance soon collapsed under the weight of infighting in mid-1979. It had lasted only two years. Indira Gandhi's Congress party regained its majority in the 1980 election, and again ruled alone until 1989. But the Janata experience was a harbinger of things to come. An opposition coalition again assumed power in 1989, only to collapse in late 1990. In 1991, India again featured a hung Parliament where no single party held a majority. This time, Congress formed a coalition of its own.

The 1991 Congress-led coalition lasted for its full five-year term, and counts as one of the most successful governments in post-independence India. Under Prime Minister PV Narashimha Rao, it undertook a series of dramatic economic reforms that liberalised the Indian economy. Rao personally tackled the infamous 'licence Raj', a set of rules and regulations that made it very difficult to do business in the country. The government boosted economic growth from only 1 per cent in 1991 to 7.55 per cent in 1996.[19] Since 1991, every national government in India has been a coalition. During the 25-year period under coalitions, economic growth has averaged 6.9 per cent a year, compared to only 4.4 per cent over the preceding 25 years when Congress enjoyed overwhelming power.[20]

Despite the fact that coalition governments oversaw the reconstruction of much of Europe following World War Two, and relative successes like India, the story of coalition governance is not always a happy one. Closer to home, the recent case of Kenya[21] embodies much of the promise and perils inherent to coalition governance.

The Kenyan story started off with great promise. After nearly

40 years of authoritarian single-party rule under Daniel arap Moi's Kenya African National Union (KANU) – Kenya's resident liberation movement – the country dramatically transitioned to democracy when Moi's chosen successor, Uhuru Kenyatta, lost the 2002 presidential election.

In December 2002, KANU was defeated by a pre-election alliance, dubbed the National Rainbow Coalition (NARC), which brought together all major opposition leaders under one umbrella. NARC's presidential candidate, Mwai Kibaki, resoundingly defeated KANU's Kenyatta by a margin of 61.3 per cent to 30.2 per cent. It was a monumental achievement in a country that had never before known democracy. The election result lit the flame of hope in Kenya, a nation of about 35 million people at the time, with NARC promising to introduce a new, more democratic Constitution. But problems soon emerged within the coalition government. Contrary to his pre-election pledge, Kibaki quickly sidelined his coalition partner, Raila Odinga, by refusing to give Odinga's faction half of the ministerial positions in cabinet.

Tensions continued to build over Kibaki's apparent betrayal. Contrary to NARC's pre-election pledges, Kibaki proposed a new Constitution that would further centralise and entrench presidential powers. Fearing a presidential power grab, Odinga's faction revolted. In the build-up to a countrywide referendum in which Kenyans would vote on whether to adopt Kibaki's proposed new Constitution, Odinga's camp openly campaigned against the president. Odinga's group won, as 58 per cent of voters rejected the new Constitution. Furious at the outcome, Kibaki dismissed his entire cabinet, and the coalition collapsed. The failure of the coalition dashed the hopes of millions of Kenyans. Instead of a new dawn, Kibaki's government overpowered Odinga's faction and simply decided that 'It's Our Turn to Eat'.[22]

But the worst was still to come, as former coalition partners Kibaki and Odinga directly faced off against one another during the 2007 presidential election. When election day finally arrived in December 2007, early Parliamentary results indicated that Odinga's newly formed party, the Orange Democratic Movement (ODM), had won 99 seats against Kibaki's Party of National Unity's (PNU) 43, but the number of seats won by other parties that also supported Kibaki made the split almost even.[23] The race for the presidency was even closer. Despite polls initially showing Odinga to be in the lead, the electoral commission eventually declared Kibaki the winner by a margin of 46 per cent to 44 per cent, with six other candidates capturing the balance.[24]

Amid widespread claims of electoral irregularities, the announcement of Kibaki's victory immediately unleashed violence between the two opposing camps. The unrest quickly spread and assumed an ethnic dimension, as supporters of the two candidates attacked people from communities supposedly associated with the rival party.[25] During a period of two months, fighting between Kibaki supporters and Odinga supporters claimed more than 1 200 lives, and displaced some 350 000 people.[26] What had once been a dream of co-operative democratic renewal had turned into a zero-sum nightmare, as Kenya faced its greatest crisis since gaining independence in 1963.

Under the auspices of a group of African leaders led by former UN Secretary-General Kofi Annan, the two parties negotiated for 41 tense days, finally striking a coalition peace deal on 28 February 2008. Under the agreement, Kibaki retained the presidency and Odinga became prime minister, a newly created position. Kenyans dubbed the arrangement the grand coalition. The sombre atmosphere that characterised the inauguration of Kenya's second successive coalition cabinet was very different from the hopeful atmosphere that had filled the air after the 2002 election.

Facing even higher stakes, and backed by an internationally mediated coalition agreement that included a detailed list of action items, Kenya's grand coalition proved to be more successful than the first NARC coalition. Most significantly, the coalition drafted a new Constitution that was approved by 68.60 per cent of voters in a 2010 referendum. The Kenya National Reconciliation and Dialogue (KNDR), an independent monitoring project established by Annan's office, concluded that the event marked 'a major turning point in Kenya's history', and that 'the new Constitution is of monumental historical significance to Kenya and even to Africa in general'.[27]

Despite serious infighting during the first two years, the grand coalition also adopted the 2011 Judicial Service Commission Act, which sought to streamline the functioning of legal and judicial institutions, and an additional law that authorised a system for vetting judges. Under a new chief justice, the court system became more transparent. Similarly, the parties in Parliament amended standing orders in order to make legislative proceedings more transparent and to create departmental oversight committees. A January 2013 public opinion survey found that 72 per cent of respondents approved of the grand coalition's performance.[28] Nevertheless, the coalition achieved little in the fight against corruption, and also failed to fundamentally reform the civil service.

On India's northern border, the Himalayan nation of Nepal[29] provides another powerful example of how the inability to compromise, combined with the pure pursuit of self-interest, can destroy a fledgling coalition-based polity. Following the 2006 end of a decade-long civil war that claimed about 17 000 lives and displaced 100 000 people,[30] a burgeoning pro-democracy movement in this country of 27 million people led the warring Maoist rebels to reach a peace agreement with the traditionalist Nepali Congress Party. Following the peace deal, Nepal abolished its 239-year-old monarchy, and held its first democratic election for a constituent assembly in April 2008. With an assembly in place to write a new Constitution, Nepalese citizens were hopeful that the country was on the cusp of a great transformation.

But the 2008 election produced a hung Parliament. Because no party held a majority, a coalition among political parties was necessary in order to form a government. From 2008 to 2012, Nepal had four different prime ministers heading four different coalition cabinets (one of which consisted of no less than 22 different parties). Under these circumstances, drafting a new Constitution proved an insurmountable challenge. Unable to agree on terms, Nepal's constituent assembly was dissolved on 27 May 2012. The country still did not have a new Constitution.

This plunged the country into a constitutional crisis that could be resolved only through fresh elections. But animosity between different groups ran so deep that the parties were unable to form a government to even organise the elections. After months of deadlock and disagreement, the only option left was to create a non-political interim government that would hold new elections. Desperate to find a way out of the impasse, political leaders took the extraordinary step of asking the country's chief justice, Khil Raj Regmi, to oversee a temporary government that would organise the elections. The interim government managed to hold the frayed country together, and conducted relatively successful elections for a new constituent assembly in November 2013.

On 20 September 2015, almost a decade after the end of the civil war, Nepal's divided government finally adopted a new Constitution. But the new legal framework did little to address the extreme levels of partisan deadlock in Nepali politics and society. Between October 2015 and June 2017, Nepal again had three different coalition governments. In total, the country had 10 different coalition cabinets between 2008 and 2017. Since 2008, the average Nepali coalition has lasted for only 337 days.

Returning to the global perspective, the fact that a majority of developed nations also regularly feature coalition governments indicates that there is indeed some correlation between Lijphart-type co-operative democracy and prosperity. The cases of Germany and India also provide some tantalising indications that the relationship might be causal. In other words, inclusive coalition governments *could* be better at creating prosperity than single-party ones, although much more research needs to be done before we can reach a firmer conclusion.

For the purposes of this book, the key takeaway is that many societies, including deeply fragmented ones such as post-Cold War Germany and post-independence India (and, to a lesser extent, post-KANU Kenya) have made real progress under coalitions. It is therefore not true that the relative instability which accompanies coalition governance necessarily inhibits development. But it is also possible that coalitions can empower would-be demagogues (as with Kibaki in Kenya), or lead to total political deadlock (as in Nepal). This variation in outcomes suggests that there are other factors at play which influence whether any given coalition survives, and whether it is able to engineer greater prosperity.

The hopeful conclusion is that political leaders and society at large have the power to make coalitions work. If political parties are able to engineer compromises on the basis of clearly defined values, and if the coalition operates in a society that understands and accepts the complex dynamics inherent to the coalition form, then it may well provide a more inclusive foundation for prosperity than single-party majoritarianism.

Three futures

Based on the experiences of other coalition-based societies, the next section introduces three scenarios of what it could mean in practice when coalitions become the norm in South Africa. These three scenarios do not constitute the sum total of all possible futures. By definition, one of the core features of coalition-based polities is that they are much more unpredictable than countries dominated by only one or two political parties. It is plainly impossible to envisage *all* of the different potential permutations that await South Africa.

Looking across the country's 226 local municipalities, 44 district municipalities, eight metropolitan municipalities and nine provinces, it is likely that there will soon be dozens of different political combinations in charge of local, municipal and national governments. As politics becomes more competitive, the influence of independent candidates, especially in municipalities, will become yet another important factor that introduces even more uncertainty. It goes far beyond the scope of this book to examine every possible coalition combination across South Africa's 288 different elected governments (278 municipalities, nine provinces, and one national).

Instead, we will stick to the national level, with each of the scenarios only briefly touching on some of the potential effects at the subnational level. (If the ANC does indeed lose Gauteng in 2019, the quest to build a coalition government in that province will be the most vivid example of how the challenges outlined in the three national-level scenarios are also relevant to provinces and municipalities.)

Even if we largely focus on the national level, predicting how a government will be constituted is about to get exponentially more complex. Previously, as soon as national election results were announced, South Africans immediately knew who their next president would be. But once the ANC vote drops below 50 per cent, citizens will need to wait for up to 30 days to find out who will become the next president (the Constitution allows up to 30 days for the National Assembly to elect one of its members as president).

The 30 days following the 2019 election could be one of the most decisive periods since 1994. With ANC support below 50 per cent, political parties would need to use these 30 days to cobble together a coalition to take over the national government. Based on the electoral trends outlined in part one of this book, there would likely be only three potentially realistic outcomes.

In the first scenario, the DA and EFF (and potentially one or two smaller parties, including an ANC breakaway) establish a coalition that leaves the ANC out of power. In the second, the ANC and EFF (maybe with one or two smaller parties) build a coalition that leaves the DA out of power. In the third, the disagreements among parties are so stark that they are unable to work together to create a formal alliance. Instead, political leaders haggle over each and every decision, including the election of the president.

It is also important to explain briefly why a fourth scenario that is theoretically possible – that of an ANC-DA coalition – will *not* happen. There is no rule that prevents the ANC and DA from establishing a 'grand coalition' after 2019. Indeed, many countries, notably Germany, regularly feature coalition governments that include the two biggest parties. Politically, the strongest argument in favour of such an arrangement is that it usually accommodates a large majority of voters. This gives such grand coalitions a high degree of legitimacy.

South Africa may in fact feature a grand coalition at some point during the 2020s. For example, if the ANC's fall in 2019 is the motivation it needs to finally reform itself from a liberation movement into a modern political party, we might even see a DA-ANC grand coalition as early as 2024. But given the country's current political atmosphere – in which the ANC is fundamentally tainted by corruption and maladministration, and part of the DA's *raison d'être* is to prove that it can out-govern the ANC – it is near impossible that the DA would risk entering an alliance with the ANC in the short term. We can safely disregard the possibility of an ANC-DA coalition in 2019.

This leaves us with the three scenarios outlined above. The first, in which DA and EFF leaders muster the maturity needed to keep a diverse alliance together, holds the greatest short-term promise for fixing South Africa. The second, in which the EFF 'returns' to the ANC via a post-2019 coalition, unleashes the populist demons that have long barked at the gates of South Africa's democracy. In the third scenario, in which none of the ANC, DA or EFF are able to form a coalition in 2019, South Africa effectively grinds to a halt under the weight of political deadlock.

There is nothing deterministic about these three scenarios. Instead, each is based on certain *probabilities*. The weight of probability does not guarantee that a DA-EFF or ANC-EFF coalition will not become deadlocked and paralysed. Neither does it mean that a DA-EFF coalition will be insulated against populism and corruption, or that an ANC-EFF alliance can never enact pragmatic policy solutions.

What probability does mean is that, based on the evidence that has accumulated in the build-up to 2019, a DA-EFF alliance is *most likely* to undertake the deep structural reforms the country needs. In turn, of the three options, an ANC-EFF coalition is *most likely* to deepen the populist and corrupt practices that have already brought South Africa to its knees. Finally, a minority government is *most likely* to be mired in incessant infighting. In the coalition era, there will be even less certainty about what the future may hold. But that does not preclude us from weighing up the evidence to make informed forecasts about what each possible future is likely to look like.

By examining the different parties' policy documents and election manifestos, the next section explores what different coalition configurations could mean for government policy on some of the most hotly contested issues in South African society, including land reform, education, economic policy, and civil service reform. More than anything else, the goal behind these three scenarios is to motivate readers to start thinking through the likely implications of different political coalitions at the national level, but also in their own provinces and municipalities. The three scenarios are not intended to be the final word. Rather, the goal is to use them to start an ongoing conversation about coalitions, which will soon become the way in which South Africa is governed.

PART TWO
South Africa in 2024: three scenarios

Chapter Five

Primed for take-off

It's the year 2024, and South Africa is governed by a multiparty coalition, led by the DA and the EFF, but excluding the declining ANC. Public sector reform is under way, reducing government debt and improving service delivery. A range of reforms has revitalised the economy, resulting in higher levels of growth and reduced unemployment, poverty and inequality. Multiparty coalitions also govern at the provincial and municipal levels, promoting more effective representation of local and regional interests, as well as greater accountability. South Africa is on its way to becoming a better governed, more peaceful and more prosperous society.

Just five years ago, South Africa was mired in its deepest political and social crisis since the end of apartheid. Following its ascent to power in 1994, the ANC had become increasingly predatory and incompetent. In 2012, in a display of contempt for citizens that would be unthinkable today, the ANC's then president, Jacob Zuma, referred to critics of his administration as 'clever blacks'.[1] In the same vein, in 2013, then Gauteng premier Nomvula Mokonyane told protesting residents in the town of Bekkersdal in her province that 'people can threaten us and say they won't vote, but the ANC doesn't need their dirty votes'.[2]

Having never won less than 62 per cent of votes in a national election, the ANC disregarded warning signs like its declining vote in the 2016 municipal elections, and continued to believe it had a God-given right to govern the country. In 2015, Zuma publicly declared that, for him, 'the ANC came before South Africa'.[3]

But the ANC was in for a shock. It began with the party's spectacular electoral slide in the 2019 national and provincial elections, when voters in the Western Cape and Gauteng revolted against its poor governance and corruption. Two thirds of Western Cape voters and 60 per cent of Gauteng voters turned against the ANC. Even though the party managed to hold on to North West and the Northern Cape, its support in those provinces declined by nearly 10 per cent compared to 2014, thereby helping to push the party's share of the national vote below 50 per cent.

However, in most provinces, no single opposition party managed to reach the magical 50 per cent mark on its own. While the DA comfortably held on to its Western Cape stronghold, no single party gained a majority in Gauteng. With control of the national government as well as Gauteng in the balance, it was coalition time.

Forging a workable coalition

The ANC quickly ran into trouble. Due to its tainted political brand, the party could not find coalition partners willing to help it hang on to power. The DA had spent a quarter of a century fighting an increasingly corrupt ANC. Now that it was finally within sight of removing the ANC from power, it made no sense to party leaders to include it in a coalition that would keep it in the Union Buildings.

In line with its perceived role of kingmaker, the EFF pretended to be talking to both the ANC and the DA. However, it reached a similar conclusion to the DA. While EFF leader Julius Malema had previously hinted the party would consider working with the ANC if the latter agreed to populist policies, EFF leaders recognised that their brand had become fundamentally associated with vocal opposition to the ANC. Betraying that brand by working with the ANC at the first opportunity would alienate sections of the party's support base. If 2019 was too early to think about an ANC-DA government, it was also too early to think about an ANC-EFF alliance.

The ANC's belief in its right to rule also meant the party was woefully unprepared for the coalition era. As recently as July 2017 – less than two years before the ANC lost Gauteng and the national government – the party's head of political education, Nathi Mthethwa, still insisted that the ANC would not prepare for coalitions because that would be 'defeatist'.[4] After the 2019 results, this inability to face up to its declining popularity threw the party into chaos as it scrambled to convince the EFF or DA to join it in a coalition.

The value of preparation

While the ANC was dazed and confused, the DA and EFF sprang into action. The DA was particularly well prepared. It had a long history of navigating coalitions and political mergers. The party also actively prepared for the coalition era by undertaking a series of trips to coalition-based societies like Germany and The Netherlands in the build-up to the 2019 election. Under the steady hand of James Selfe, chairman of its federal executive, who had played a key role in managing previous DA-led mergers and alliances, the party clinched a coalition deal with the EFF and other opposition parties that gave it a Parliamentary majority. The EFF too was well prepared for the moment, having previously worked closely with the DA, and with Selfe in particular.

The relationships built among senior leaders of the DA, ACDP, COPE, FF+, UDM, IFP and EFF in places like Nelson Mandela Bay, Johannesburg and Tshwane after the 2016 municipal elections was a vital factor that helped to seal the deal. For example, while Malema initially accused the DA's mayoral candidate in Johannesburg, Herman Mashaba, of being 'anti-black',[5] the EFF ultimately helped elect Mashaba as mayor. A few months into Mashaba's term, his relationship with Malema had reportedly warmed to such a point that they regularly drank whiskey together, with Malema even saying that Mashaba could well have been an EFF member.

Coalition pact

Based on the DA's deep experience of coalitions, as well as the improved personal relationships between the parties, the first breakthrough came two weeks after the elections when the DA and EFF agreed in principle to take over the national government. They also brought on board a number of smaller parties, including the ACDP, COPE, FF+, UDM, as well as a breakaway group that had abandoned the ANC alliance. After reaching an informal agreement, the partners sought to draw up a formal coalition pact that would guide the new government's work.

It was a crucial step that took days of around-the-clock negotiations. Many media commentators speculated that the wide ideological rifts among the partners would cause the coalition to collapse almost immediately. The pressure was upped even further when the ANC tried to tempt some of the coalition partners into defecting before they had signed on the dotted line. But the ANC was just too politically toxic. The coalition held as the DA and EFF negotiators focused on putting together specific policies rather than broad ideological statements.

The next breakthrough came three weeks after the elections, when the coalition partners held a joint press conference to present their agreement to the public. It stipulated that the coalition government would operate within the confines of the South African Constitution, and would restore the independence of key state institutions such as the judiciary, prosecuting authority, Public Protector and Reserve Bank. The parties also agreed to eradicate corruption, and professionalise the civil service. In a nod to the EFF, the government committed itself to speeding up land reform by introducing a new expropriation bill, and working towards the provision of free university education up to graduate level.

Decisions by consensus

Aware of the ideological chasm among the partners, the coalition agreement also included a detailed explanation of how they planned to resolve internal disputes. First, the partners agreed that they would always try to reach decisions by consensus, particularly in cabinet. They would only vote on an issue if all other means to find a solution had failed. While the agreement discouraged coalition members from publicly criticising government decisions, it did allow partners to voice their dissatisfaction in cases where no consensus was reached, and a vote was used to break a deadlock.

Party leaders also agreed to create a coalition management committee that would meet every fortnight, and include the top five or six leaders of each party. The meetings were set up to mirror cabinet meetings, and would follow a predetermined agenda based on strict rules. Similarly, in Parliament, the whips of the coalition parties would meet every week to flag and resolve disagreements over controversial legislative proposals.

Dispute resolution

But the agreement also created space for more informal dispute resolution mechanisms. Mmusi Maimane, Malema, and other leaders each nominated one trusted political lieutenant to be in constant contact with one another. In cases where the formal forums were unable to break deadlocks, the lieutenants were tasked with brokering an agreement which they would then take to their political principals for approval. With different layers of dispute resolution built into the agreement, the top leaders would only need to step in to resolve the most serious disagreements.

Distribution of portfolios

At the joint press conference, president-elect Maimane also announced the composition of his cabinet, which was slashed from 35 to 25 ministers. This already reflected a compromise. The DA's manifesto had spoken of a government with only 15 ministries,[6] but in order to accommodate its coalition partners, the DA agreed to increase the number of portfolios to 25. The coalition had also agreed to divide ministerial portfolios among the partners according to their share of the vote. In practice, this meant the DA would control most of the powerful ministries, followed by the EFF, and then the smaller partners.

The DA ended up with the strategically important treasury,

foreign affairs, home affairs, justice, state security, police and public administration ministries, and also secured the key service delivery portfolios of public enterprises, health, and basic education. In turn, the EFF got social development, public works, co-operative governance, housing, mineral resources, and science and technology, while the smaller parties got one ministry each. The EFF secured the land reform ministry, but this was balanced out by the DA's control of the agriculture portfolio.

In order to build relationships across parties, and ensure that any given ministry did not turn into the personal fiefdom of the party that controlled it, the coalition agreed that each portfolio would get a deputy minister who belonged to a different party from the minister.

After 28 days of intense negotiations and public speculation, the National Assembly sat for the first time following the election. In the first sign that the coalition would hold, the coalition's nominee for speaker was duly elected. MPs then cast their votes for a president, with the DA's candidate triumphing over the ANC's nominee. With the ANC on the outside looking in, President Mmusi Maimane and Deputy President Julius Malema took up office in Pretoria.

Defusing initial tensions

Not unexpectedly, the process of moving into the Union Buildings created initial tensions among the partners. The first serious argument between Maimane and Malema was not over ideology or policy, but over seemingly trivial issues: the composition of their respective offices and personal staffs, and who had more cars and bodyguards.

The offices of the president and deputy president fell under the same government department, headed by the president. While Maimane was adamant that only he and the director-general could approve staff appointments in the presidency, Malema insisted that no one could tell him who to appoint in his office. Malema was also furious because Maimane had the right to more bodyguards, and to travel in more expensive cars.

The media seized on these tensions as proof that the government was about to collapse. The episode also provided the first test for the coalition's dispute resolution systems. Behind the scenes, Maimane and Malema's lieutenants sprang into action. During two weeks of negotiations, Malema's team made it clear that he felt disrespected by having less power and stature within the presidency, while the DA's team insisted that the deputy president should indeed have less of a say than the president. But the EFF rejected the argument that the DA's leader was automatically more important than the EFF's simply because the former had garnered more than twice as many votes as the latter. The EFF quickly reminded Maimane's lieutenants that he would not be in the Union Buildings if it wasn't for Malema.

The situation was defused when Maimane granted Malema sole control over appointments to his personal office, and agreed that he could hire more bodyguards. However, instead of buying more luxurious cars for the deputy president, Maimane and Malema resolved to sell some of the vehicles in the presidential fleet so that their respective convoys would comprise exactly the same type and number of vehicles. The issue was also tabled during the first fortnightly coalition management committee meeting, where the partners – alarmed by the early crisis – decided to draw up a framework for how to handle political appointments across the cabinet.

Although the coalition agreement specified that the government was committed to creating a fit-for-purpose, merit-based civil service, the dispute over appointments to Malema's personal office illustrated the need for flexibility. In response, the committee resolved that the president, deputy president, and ministers would be allowed to appoint no more than five staff members purely on the basis of 'political imperatives'.

In essence, the move exempted political advisers from the strict appointment rules that the government planned to impose on the civil service, thereby granting politicians greater flexibility to appoint staff in their personal offices. The episode was an important early example of how personal disagreements and symbolic choices could flare up into a serious dispute. But it also showed that the forums created to resolve disputes would work as long as senior leaders were willing to reach reasonable compromises.

Public sector reform
Cadre deployment abolished
Despite the early clash of personalities, the positive effects of South Africa's new coalition reality on government policy became clear shortly after the end of ANC hegemony. The most significant and immediate shift after the DA-EFF coalition assumed power was its decision to abandon the ANC's policy of cadre deployment. Through this policy, implemented from 1997 onwards, the ANC had succeeded in ensuring that loyal party members took control of almost all powerful positions in the civil service.[7]

Cadre deployment provided an easy way for ANC ministers to hand cushy, high-paying jobs to their colleagues and friends. The effects were devastating. The policy swelled the ranks of the civil service by more than a quarter during the 2000s. By 2014, an unsustainable 2.69 million people worked in the public sector.[8] This meant that nearly three out of every ten working people relied on the state for their incomes. Between 2005 and 2012, the public service wage bill ballooned by a staggering 145.6 per cent.[9] By 2017, it had exceeded R500 billion, making up about 36 per cent of the entire national budget, and equalling 2 per cent of the country's annual economic output.[10]

Cadre deployment also crippled the civil service by draining it of skills. By valuing political connections over competence or performance, the ANC packed the civil service with millions of overpaid people who were incapable of and uninterested in doing their jobs. By 2016, despite hiring hundreds of thousands of additional civil servants, public sector productivity had not improved.

Employing often incompetent party loyalists as civil servants in powerful positions where they had to decide which companies would get tenders also contributed to the wave of corruption that engulfed the country under the ANC. Long before South Africans even invented the term 'state capture' to describe the Gupta family's influence over Zuma and his cronies, the ANC had successfully captured the levers of the civil service, to the detriment of every citizen who depended on public services. The ANC's hollowing out of state capacity contributed to near daily and often violent protests against poor service delivery, and underpinned the looting that had emerged at state-owned enterprises like Eskom, Prasa, Transnet and South African Airways (SAA).

But the 2019 coalition operated in a different reality. The national government immediately ended cadre deployment, and launched a process of right-sizing and rationalising the civil service. It encouraged early retirement, froze all non-essential positions, and prohibited civil servants from doing business with the state.

The Maimane administration also enacted legislation that strengthened the once toothless Public Service Commission, which had acted as a rubber stamp under the ANC. Under the coalition, the commission became a truly independent institution with the power to approve and oversee all senior civil service appointments. (The only appointments exempted from scrutiny by the commission were the five political positions in ministers' personal offices.) It rigorously monitored all appointments to guard against political interference, and strictly enforced performance contracts, which every state employee was required to sign. Finally, it carried out a countrywide vetting and testing exercise to verify the competence and qualifications of state employees. Those who lacked the minimum requirements were required to apply for retraining, or accept retrenchment packages.

The coalition had numerous reasons for acting decisively against cadre deployment. Firstly, it had inherited a wholly unsustainable budget. The billions lost or stolen by incompetent and corrupt ANC cadres was one of the main reasons why, by 2017, the country's debt-to-GDP ratio had reached a crippling 54 per cent, the highest among its emerging market peers[11] (see Figure 8 on the next page on how government debt had ballooned under the last ANC administration). As a result, by 2019, South Africa had already endured three years of economic stagnation. Towards the end of the ANC administration, a sheer lack of funding even imperilled the government's ability to pay social grants to 17 million beneficiaries. It was clear that drastic spending cuts would have to be made, and with the civil service wage bill approaching half of all government expenditure, it was a prime candidate for downsizing.

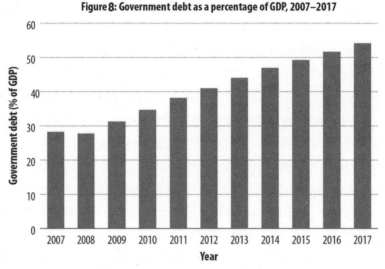

Figure 8: Government debt as a percentage of GDP, 2007–2017

Source: Trading Economics.

But the coalition also had a clear political incentive to act against cadre deployment, namely the prospect that at least some public servants deployed by the ANC would try to sabotage the new government. Just as the ANC had faced a situation at the end of apartheid where many senior civil servants were perceived to be aligned to the previous regime, the coalition had to deal with the real or perceived hostility of senior civil servants appointed by the ANC. Therefore, they had an additional reason to make them leave.

This time, however, given that no single party held power on its own, any policy similar to cadre deployment would no longer give a single party control of the state. If cadre deployment had remained in place, it would probably have been a source of conflict within the coalition, as partners would have deadlocked over whom to appoint. Attempting to take patronage out of the equation and creating a civil service that would implement all policies regardless of which coalition partner proposed it was thus seen as the best way to avoid unnecessary conflict.

Finally, it was easier to reform the civil service than many observers believed possible, because it represented an area of strong agreement within the coalition. In its 2014 manifesto, the DA declared: 'We unequivocally reject the style of cadre deployment (as espoused by the ANC [in] its strategy and tactics documents).' In 2016, the EFF manifesto also stated that 'the EFF . . . will put an end to cadre deployment practices and policies'. In a near mirror image of the DA's promise to fix the civil service by 'ensuring that appointment decisions are based on the capacity of a person to deliver on the duties of her or his office', the EFF declared that 'employees will be employed on the basis of their qualifications and suitability for the job, and not on the basis of which political party they belong [to].'[12]

Merit-based appointments

The coalition's programme to fix the state also extended to law enforcement, health care, and education. Guided by the principle of building a merit-based civil service, political leaders agreed that the security institutions should be managed by independent and competent administrators. As was the case with other civil servants, the existence of a coalition government made it more difficult for any one party to capture the security apparatus.

Politically, the appointment of independent technocrats was seen as the best possible compromise.

Maimane also appointed a professional police officer to head the South African Police Service (SAPS). With cadre deployment outlawed, and a powerful Public Service Commission overseeing all appointments, the police service was on the road to professionalisation.

National Prosecuting Authority and the Scorpions

Similarly competent appointments were made at the NPA. The coalition also quickly resolved to bring back the former Directorate of Special Operations (DSO), commonly known as the Scorpions. Formed by then president Mbeki in 2001, the Zuma administration disbanded it in 2009, presumably to protect corrupt policemen and politicians within the then governing party against investigation and criminal prosecution. Once re-established, one of the crime-busting unit's first moves was to pursue corruption and treason charges against Jacob Zuma and his top officials.

Health

In the midst of the budget crisis inherited from the ANC, the coalition government also suspended plans to implement a national health insurance system, which was estimated to cost between R256 and R367 billion by 2025.[13] After years of economic stagnation and worsening public debt, the country simply did not have the money. However, the EFF publicly declared that it opposed this decision, and would continue to push for a national health insurance system.

While the coalition partners disagreed about universal insurance, they strongly agreed about the need to improve public health services. Since health care was a shared competence between the national and provincial governments, the national coalition did not have the power to manage each hospital in the country directly. Instead, they focused on using their regulatory powers to fix the system. The first step was to vet the payrolls and qualifications of all doctors, nurses and other health care providers working in state institutions. This exercise uncovered high levels of fraud and an acute lack of skills in many public hospitals.

In response, the health ministry launched a nationwide retraining programme for all public health workers, while the Public Service Commission reviewed the competence of hospital administrators. In cases where managers lacked the necessary skills, they were offered retrenchment packages and were replaced by suitably qualified administrators. Although the private insurance market was allowed to continue, the government implemented stricter regulations for medical aid schemes in order to curb the costs of private care. It also established a partnership programme that offered financial incentives for private hospitals to team up with public institutions. Under the partnership arrangement, officials from private hospitals were seconded to public institutions and vice versa, enabling the transfer of management and other skills.

Education

A critical lack of skills in the health care sector, as well as in many other economic spheres, undermined productivity and economic growth. The coalition's next urgent task was to reform the public education system. The waves of student protests that had rocked the country in the lead-up to the 2019 election were high on the public agenda. The coalition declared higher education funding a national priority, and immediately replaced the entire senior leadership of the woefully inefficient National Student Financial Aid Scheme (NSFAS). Using funding redirected from failing SOEs such as SAA, the government undertook to fund all undergraduate students from families earning less than R600 000 a year. In a nod to the EFF's campaign promise, the coalition sold the reform as the introduction of 'free education up to the undergraduate level'.

But the biggest crisis lay in the basic education sector. In the ANC era, South Africa's schools were rated as among the worst in the world, ranking 75th out of 76 in a 2015 study.[14] This was despite the fact that the government spent 15 per cent of its entire budget on education – more than the United States, Germany, and many other countries.[15] The problem was clearly not a lack of resources.

The basic education crisis was nothing short of a national scandal. As the largest employer of workers paid by the state, the education sector had become the poster child for cadre deployment and corruption. The first problem was that many teachers were unqualified, and did not belong anywhere near a classroom. For example, in 2015, more than half of all grade R teachers did not hold the qualification required by their position.[16] Although numbers were hard to come by and were inherently untrustworthy due to corruption, the coalition assumed correctly that tens of thousands out of the country's 400 000 teachers were underqualified, and unsuited to their posts.

Endemic corruption was the second problem that had crippled education and robbed children of their futures. The extent of the rot was vividly exposed in a 2016 ministerial task team report into the buying and selling of teacher posts, commonly referred to as the 'jobs-for-cash report'. It laid bare the outrageous levels of corruption fostered by the ANC. The report revealed that all the deputy directors-general in the department of basic education were members of the South African Democratic Teachers Union (SADTU), and attended union meetings. Furthermore, it quoted the Gauteng member of the executive committee for education as stating that the major teachers' union, SADTU, was in charge of education in his province, while the head of the North West education department lamented that his department had information on so many cases of wrongdoing that if he asked the police to follow them up, it would amount to closing down the department.[17]

In order to tackle these and other ills, the coalition's education ministry launched a project to test and vet the skills and qualifications of all South Africa's public school teachers. The project was fiercely resisted by SADTU, the teachers' union that had turned the education system into its own fiefdom. In provinces where SADTU's grip was particularly strong, hundreds of schools came to a standstill as teachers protested against having to take some of the same tests they expected their learners to pass. The crisis eventually ended when a court ruled that the state indeed had the authority to vet its workforce. Although some schools were closed for months, the vast majority of teachers eventually participated in the vetting exercise. Importantly, in exchange for allowing it to claim credit for the introduction of free higher education, the EFF agreed to support the teacher clean-up exercise tacitly despite its ideologically grounded sympathy for labour unions.

The tests revealed that there were thousands of 'ghost teachers' on the state's payroll. Removing them immediately saved millions of rands which could be employed more productively elsewhere. The project also revealed that tens of thousands of teachers did not have the required qualifications. Some were retrained, while others were retrenched. With SADTU having been dealt a painful blow, and amidst massive public blowback from parents against the union's intransigence, the education ministry adopted strict rules that prohibited ministry officials who were not employed as teachers from joining SADTU. The ministry also hired more superintendents at the provincial and local levels, tasked with strictly supervising teachers.

Land reform

The coalition government also made significant progress on land reform. Although this remained the biggest area of disagreement among the different partners, it also became a prominent example of how co-operation could result in unexpected productive compromises.

The EFF insisted that the department of land reform – which was headed by an EFF minister – should introduce a new law that would make it easier to expropriate land for redistribution. In a key compromise, the DA agreed, on condition that all expropriation should happen subject to the Constitution's call for 'just and equitable' compensation.

While the EFF was opposed in principle to the DA's stipulation, it quickly recognised that two thirds of MPs were unlikely to support an amendment to the Constitution's property clause. The EFF was also bound by the coalition agreement, which required all partners to abide by the Constitution as it stood (including section 25, which enshrined the right to private property). With the DA apparently willing to talk about the land issue, the EFF was careful not to push too hard and risk collapsing the coalition.

A comprehensive legislative compromise slowly developed as a new expropriation bill made its way through Parliament. Politically, the DA handed the EFF a key win when it supported the bill's adoption. This enabled the EFF to claim credibly that it had finally made the expropriation of 'white-owned land' a reality. Whereas the 'willing buyer, willing seller' model previously meant that the government could not force anyone to sell their land even if they were offered a reasonable price, the state could now force a land owner to sell at a fair price. But the legislation also established an independent land tribunal to which land owners could turn if they felt they had not received just and equitable compensation. Importantly, when a dispute arose, the state could not take possession of expropriated land before the independent tribunal made its ruling.

Whereas the DA's opening position could be crudely summarised as 'no expropriation', and the EFF's as 'expropriation without any compensation,' the imperatives of coalition government meant that the two parties eventually settled on a compromise of 'expropriation with reasonable compensation'. Because the new bill incorporated an independent mechanism to ensure that property owners were fairly compensated when their land was expropriated, it passed constitutional muster. The compromise also set the tone for how the coalition partners communicated controversial decisions to their supporters, with the parties organising regular media conferences to explain the rationale behind the policy choices.

With a framework in place to speed up the process of acquiring existing agricultural land for redistribution, the government also focused on empowering beneficiaries to use land productively. The partners agreed that more had to be done to empower the millions of people living on 'communal' land in South Africa's ten former homelands as well as 27 smaller former 'coloured reserves'. Under former ANC administrations, South Africans living in communal areas were left to languish as the ANC chose to empower chiefs over citizens.

When the DA-EFF coalition assumed power in 2019, more than 16 million people – almost all of whom were black – were living on 17.2 million hectares of communal land.[18] This was equal to over 20 per cent of the 82 million hectares used for commercial agriculture. But many lived in dire poverty. Over 90 per cent of the country's poorest municipal wards were located in former homelands, while more than 73 per cent of people living on communal land earned less than R604 a month (mostly from social grants), compared to 46 per cent for the rest of the country.[19] While communal areas in the east of the country, such as the former Transkei and Ciskei, contained some of South Africa's most fertile agricultural land, almost none of it was under cultivation. The 16 million inhabitants of the former homelands sat on land with enormous agricultural potential, which could serve as the country's breadbasket.

The problem was that people in communal areas did not own their land. Even though the ANC had initially promised to transfer communal land to the people, it had quickly reneged on that promise. Instead, successive ANC administrations empowered unelected traditional leaders, giving them de facto ownership of all communal land. As in feudal Europe, no farmer on communal land was willing to invest in their farming operations when the local chief could simply confiscate their produce or land at any moment. In return, the chiefs were expected to force their 'subjects' into voting for the ANC.

Besides genuine concerns over the need to empower people living in the former homelands, the DA-EFF coalition had a good political reason to act. With the ANC roundly defeated in the urban provinces of the Western Cape and Gauteng, it was clear that it had largely been reduced to a party of poor, rural people. Given the ANC's control over rural patronage networks, the former homelands were some of its biggest remaining strongholds. But since land reform was a national government responsibility, the ANC would no longer be able to promote the interests of the chiefs over those of rural dwellers.

The coalition partners agreed that they needed to move ownership of communal land away from traditional leaders, but the DA and EFF clashed on how to go about it. Whereas the DA favoured individual ownership, with rural dwellers receiving freehold title deeds to individual parcels of land, the EFF preferred collective state ownership.

After months of haggling, the partners eventually agreed to another compromise. As a first step, the government passed legislation that vested ownership of communal land in the former homelands in elected communal property associations. Although chiefs could be elected to the associations, they would not have any veto powers. The new law required communities to define themselves and elect leaders to an executive committee, which would decide on the allocation of land use rights. Crucially, the entire community had to be consulted on any decision to allow someone to use a piece of land. In collaboration with local deeds offices, the committees were also required to maintain a detailed land registry.

The government undertook a programme to survey and map every parcel of land in the communal areas. It also launched a massive awareness campaign aimed at informing members of rural communities about their rights to own the land they were living on and using. At the end of the process, each self-defined communal property association received an official title deed and survey map that clearly demarcated the outer boundary of the communal land. Within the community, elected committees were responsible for issuing occupancy certificates to individual households. In a slight modification of a call introduced in the EFF's founding manifesto, the national government also resolved to supply more than half of all hospitals, schools, prisons and other public institutions within 100 kilometres of communal areas with food purchased from smallholder farmers.[20]

Although the DA was not entirely satisfied and resolved to keep pushing for a system of individual ownership, and the EFF would have preferred greater state control, the compromise position finally broke the stranglehold of unaccountable traditional authorities. Communities in the former homelands now had democratic control over their land, and with constant support from the deeds office and the land reform ministry, they were able to maintain land registries that provided greater security of tenure. With communal property rights secured, the once fallow fields of the former home-lands were beginning to transform into productive farms.

Alongside faster redistribution under the expropriation law, the tenure reform process in communal areas meant that the coalition government had drastically increased black ownership over productive land from only 7 per cent in 2017 to well over 30 per cent by 2024. Working together, the coalition reached the 30 per cent mark within five short years – a goal which the ANC had failed to achieve for more than 25 years.

Mining

The coalition engineered similar compromise solutions in other areas. The EFF initially pushed for the nationalisation of the country's mines, while the DA was opposed to nationalisation. The coalition government then launched a commission to investigate and propose possible changes to South Africa's mining tax and royalty system. It found that mining companies were already paying heavy taxes, but that those funds could be better managed. In response, the government imposed stricter tax collection rules, and ring-fenced much of the money generated from mining activities. The mining fund was used to directly benefit mining communities across the country.

Housing

Another example was housing, where the government worked with municipalities to use the new expropriation law to their advantage. Under the ANC, one of the reasons why municipalities had long struggled to extend better services into informal settlements was that many of those settlements were illegally built on land owned by private individuals or other state entities. The key was to regularise and legally recognise those settlements.[21]

With about 13 per cent of South Africans, equal to 2.2 million households, still living in informal settlements,[22] the national housing department undertook an audit of peri-urban land around all major towns and cities with the goal of buying or expropriating (with compensation) some of the land upon which urban informal settlements were built. This enabled municipalities to install services legally, whereafter the land could be subdivided, titled, and transferred to the occupants. This policy, commonly known as in-situ upgrading, again reflected an interim position between the EFF's purely statist goals and the DA's more market-based ideals.

While continuing to build state-subsidised houses for low-income earners (albeit on a reduced scale, due to the budget crisis), the coalition ramped up delivery of serviced housing sites. Under this model, the government cleared and subdivided municipal land, installed basic services such as water, electricity and sewerage, and then allocated erven to people in the so-called gap market (those who earned too little to buy land, but too much to qualify for a free house).

It also provided subsidies to municipalities to form partnerships with community-driven housing developments. The strategic focus on serviced sites to complement subsidised housing was another point of synergy between the DA and EFF, with the latter having pledged in 2014 that 'the EFF's people municipality will provide housing stands with basic services, and allocate them for free to people who need to build houses for them-selves'.[23]

Economic reform

Above all, digging the country out of the hole sunk by the ANC required jump-starting its moribund economy. While the DA, as the senior partner in the coalition, was happy to agree to some of the EFF's demands about land reform and higher education, it stuck to its guns when it came to economic reforms. With the finance ministry under its control, the DA put its foot down.

Investor confidence

The administration's first task was to regain international investor confidence. Capitalising on the international goodwill generated by a peaceful change of government, the coalition affirmed the independence of vital institutions such as the Reserve Bank. (The DA did, however, throw the EFF a political bone by buying back the Reserve Bank shares held by 660 private shareholders, allowing the latter party to claim that the bank had been 'nationalised' even though private shareholders had never had a say in the bank's policy decisions.)

Review of SOEs

Given the extent of the debt crisis, the government had to act quickly to free itself from the burden of failing SOEs. SAA, for example, was losing more than R4.5 billion a year, and South African taxpayers were sinking tens of billions of rands into keeping it afloat. In line with the ANC's cadre deployment strategy, the country's 717 SOEs had been turned into patronage machines, with well-paid senior management positions reserved for cronies irrespective of their competence.

The coalition administration addressed this by launching a comprehensive review of all 717 SOEs. The cabinet then retained state ownership of those entities that were economically viable, but reviewed all senior management appointments, and replaced ANC sycophants with appropriately qualified and experienced managers. The newly empowered Public Service Commission reviewed and approved all new appointments.

In the cases of parastatals that were deemed non-viable, such as SAA, the cabinet opted for partial privatisation. This approach provoked fierce opposition from the EFF, which made its displeasure publicly known, as allowed by the coalition agreement. But the DA held firm, and the decision to privatise some state assets was one of few instances when cabinet members voted on an issue when they could not reach consensus. The DA's motion prevailed, and the government began to sell either minority or majority stakes in many SOEs, which now had to make a profit or flounder. This ended their constant drain of taxpayer funds, and generated welcome once-off cash injections into the public purse.

Skills development

The next step was to improve skills development. Broadly following the German model, the coalition introduced a countrywide apprenticeship programme that subsidised employers which trained young people emerging from the schooling system to become mechanics, plumbers, boilermakers and electricians. The state also invested heavily in technical colleges, including

teacher and nursing training colleges, which incorporated com-
pulsory apprenticeship programmes designed to streamline the
transition into employment.

Based on a cross-party agreement that Black Economic Empowerment (BEE) should be reformed to benefit the general public
rather than a narrow ANC-connected elite, the coalition launched
an 'opportunity fund'. Budding entrepreneurs who could not
access finance elsewhere were invited to submit business plans
to the fund, where experienced business people evaluated the
ideas and granted them seed money to turn the proposals into
businesses. While the fund's scoring system assigned additional
BEE points to black applicants, it did not judge applicants' business ideas solely on the basis of their race.

Labour market reforms

With more efficient public enterprises delivering better infrastructure, a vocational training system absorbing more unemployed
people, and an opportunity fund providing support to bona fide
black businesses, the government turned its attention to labour
market reforms. The labour ministry changed employment laws
and regulations to make it easier to hire talented employees and
to fire underperforming ones. It also changed collective bargaining laws to allow workers to vote in secret on whether or not to
go on strike. While labour unions such as Cosatu were opposed
to the reforms, years of serving the bidding of the ANC had
turned the labour movement into a shadow of its former self, and
the reforms ultimately passed.

The collective bargaining system was also decentralised. Previously, wage agreements reached between a handful of large

employers and a few powerful unions were binding on an entire industry. This often severely disadvantaged smaller employers who could not afford to pay the same wages as large corporations. Under the new, decentralised system, individual companies could negotiate wage increases they could actually afford, while multiple unions were allowed to gain recognition within the same sector.

Local and provincial government

The electoral revolution triggered by the 2019 election was not limited to national government. With the ANC's myth of invincibility shattered, the former governing party's decline also continued at the local level. In the 2021 municipal polls, the ANC's nationwide support fell to 40 per cent as it lost its majorities in one town after another. By the mid-2020s, it was commonplace for analysts to compare the ANC's accelerating decline to that of its predecessor: just as the NP had fallen apart in the 1990s when it lost its aura of nationalist invincibility, so too was the ANC in free fall in the 2020s.

In 2024, travelling across South Africa's urban landscapes and vast rural spaces, the effect of the pluralisation of power was beginning to become obvious. With the ANC having lost its dominance, local issues had suddenly become much more politically salient. It might have been delayed for a quarter of a century, but South Africa was finally beginning to reflect the old cliché that all politics is local.

Language issues

For instance, in rural Namaqualand, local coalition governments that included Khoisan interest groups added the Khoekhoe language (also known as Nama) to the teaching programmes in local schools, while the Northern Cape provincial government advocated that Khoekhoe be declared an official language. In the Western Cape, pressure from local and provincial governments eventually forced Stellenbosch University to restore Afrikaans as an indigenous academic language alongside English in a province where half of the residents spoke Afrikaans as a first language. In Gauteng, where the ANC had lost power in 2019, the University of Pretoria came under pressure from the provincial government to promote local languages like Sepedi equally. Similar movements to promote regional languages and culture were emerging in provinces like the North West, where the ANC hung on by a thread.

Demographic representation

With municipal and provincial governments increasingly focusing on local rather than national issues, the grip of demographic determinism on the country's politics also began to loosen. The ANC government had concentrated on enforcing national demographic representation in every sphere of South African society. This was encapsulated in the infamous statement by Mzwanele 'Jimmy' Manyi, then director-general of labour, in March 2010 that coloured people were 'over concentrated' in the Western Cape, and should spread throughout the rest of the country.[24] His remarks came in the wake of a court case against the then-government's rigid enforcement of national demographics in public sector employment. It provoked a fierce reaction as it harked back to the forced removals of coloured communities in the apartheid era.

But Manyi's attitude was no exception. In its approach to public employment equity, the ANC government had long turned a blind eye to regional demographic variations. In some cases, ministries controlled by the national government, such as the police, flatly refused to employ coloured people in the Western Cape even when they could not find any suitable black candidates. Instead of going against the dogma of national demographic representation, ministries would often leave posts vacant rather than appoint an applicant from a minority group – even in areas where coloured, white or Indian people constituted a local majority.[25] It was a blatantly discriminatory practice that contributed to the collapse of service delivery under the ANC. The party was able to ignore local demographic variations because of its sheer political dominance.

Local interests and culture

Fortunately, the dawn of the coalition era in 2019 also brought a greater focus on regionalism. In order to win the co-operation of municipalities and provinces that increasingly sought to protect and promote local culture and interests, the national coalition government amended the employment equity legislation to the effect that greater weight would be given to regional rather than national demographics in appointments to any municipal, provincial or national government departments as well as SOEs. It was a far more equitable approach that took account of the people actually living in any given area.

Greater accountability

Although the DA had long been opposed to the ANC's obsession with national demographics, the true impetus for change came in intensified political competition at the municipal and provincial levels. The shift in educational policy to acknowledge the importance of regional languages as well as the amendments to employment equity legislation to incorporate local demographic realities were emblematic of a wider evolution in the country's political culture. Despite the fact that the electoral framework continued to undermine accountability by not allowing for the election of national and provincial representatives in geographically defined constituencies, greater political competition forced politicians to take local and regional issues more seriously.

Additionally, the country's municipal electoral system continued to include geographic constituencies (known as wards). While half of all municipal councillors were elected in terms of proportional representation, the other half were directly elected to serve a particular geographic location. Due to the greater local accountability built into the system, municipalities became especially responsive to local problems once the country's politics became more competitive. Instead of assessing political party performance based largely on loyalty to a *national* cause (as had been the case under the ANC), voters now looked to practical improvements in their *local* communities to judge governance performance. This altitudinal shift greatly improved political accountability, and fostered a closer focus on regional issues.

A society transformed

Improved service delivery

By 2024, South Africans were becoming used to having a range of different coalition governments in charge at the municipal, provincial, and national levels. The country was fast becoming unrecognisable from the one that had teetered on the edge of implosion in 2019. Thanks to the strengthening of the Public Service Commission and the introduction of merit-based public sector appointments, the state was able to improve service delivery significantly. Via voluntary retrenchments, the government also managed to reduce the number of civil servants from 2.69 million to 1.9 million.

The public sector wage bill had declined from 36 per cent of the total annual budget in 2017 to a much healthier 28 per cent in 2024. Those remaining on the public payroll, including health workers and teachers, were vetted and tested to ensure that they were able to do their jobs properly. The public tasted the fruits. South Africa's international education rating was improving, hospitals were better managed, infrastructure was maintained and improved, and the crime rate declined.

Creating a leaner and more efficient civil service freed up space in the budget. Although the country was still mired in debt, by the end of the coalition's term in 2024, debt servicing costs were declining. Combined with structural reforms that resulted in higher foreign direct investment inflows, South Africa's economy managed to escape the recession engineered by Jacob Zuma's government and was now growing at a healthy 5 per cent a year.

During the Zuma years between 2009 and 2017, South Africa's ranking on the World Bank's *Doing Business* index had plummeted from 32nd to 74th.[26] After 2019, however, driven by the coalition's reforms, it improved to 25th by 2024. Unemployment also declined from 27.7 per cent in 2017 to 21 per cent in 2024.

In a powerful endorsement of the successes achieved by South Africa's first national coalition government, the major credit rating agencies returned the country to investment grade. South Africans were getting richer, as GDP per capita increased to \$16 000 from only \$12 260 in 2016.[27] Inequality also declined moderately, with the country's score on the Gini index moving from about 0.63 to 0.59 (on the Gini index, a lower score denotes lower equality, while a higher score indicates greater inequality).

Co-operation and compromise

The country's progress was driven by the continual co-operation and compromise required by coalitions. In order to stay in power, members of coalition governments not only had to retain the respect of voters, but also had to protect and nurture the relationships with their coalition partners. With the likelihood of winning 50 per cent of the vote at any level of government rapidly decreasing, political parties knew they needed to work together if they wanted to be in power. To work together, they had to compromise. This did not mean that politics were necessarily any less fiery – indeed, the relationship between the coalition partners grew tense towards the end of the government's term as parties positioned themselves for the 2024 election. There were still no permanent friends in politics.

Although coalitions at the municipal level often shifted according to fluid by-election results, or where serious disputes arose, political leaders quickly grew to understand that these were the new rules of the game. Whereas party discipline could be quite easily enforced when only one party was in power, it was impossible to discipline another party's members. By developing clear new coalition norms and rules of engagement, political leaders managed to form relatively stable governments despite the shifting complexions of some coalitions.

A new role for citizens

Their efforts were bolstered by South African citizens, who quickly internalised the new rules of the game. They grew to understand that the set of circumstances they had become used to during the first two-and-a-half decades of democracy were exceptional. Under the country's proportional representation system, it was highly unlikely that any one party would gain a dominant upper hand over all the others. The ANC's dominance after 1994 merely attested to the exceptional power the party's liberation narrative had initially wielded over voters. Voters understood that this singular and unique message, born of the struggle against apartheid, was indeed powerful enough to overwhelm the electoral system's tendency towards fragmentation. But they also knew that the message had slowly lost its lustre until it was buried under an avalanche of corruption and misery.

Where they had once thought in terms of clear distinctions between the 'ruling party' and everyone else, South Africans now understood that those old boundaries had faded. A party with almost no support in one region could easily be the dominant force in a neighbouring area, and could simultaneously be a junior partner in a broad national coalition government.

More importantly, voters realised that values-based compromise had become the basic requirement for any government to implement any of its promises. Election manifestos were no longer perceived as being set in stone. Instead, they were essentially part of a complex set of negotiations between parties and voters, and among different political leaders. Compromising on part of a manifesto in order to achieve the best possible outcome under any given coalition arrangement was not labelled as a sell-out.

As long as it was based on values in line with the Constitution, and communicated effectively to voters, compromise came to be seen as the oil that greased the gears of the country's plural and vibrant coalition-based democracy.

As voters lined up for the 2024 election amid intense speculation about which parties would partner up to form the next national coalition government, South Africa was primed for take-off.

Chapter Six

A toxic homecoming

It's the year 2024, and South Africa is governed by an ANC-EFF coalition that unexpectedly won power in 2019. In exchange for keeping the ANC in power, the EFF has forced its formerly dominant coalition partner to adopt a range of populist policies, including expropriation of land and mines without compensation. It has also joined the ANC in looting the state; patronage has been extended, and corruption has worsened. Following a loss of investor confidence as well as undue government intervention and mismanagement, the economy is in a downward spiral, and South Africa's democracy is under siege.

Looking back on the five years since the 2019 national elections, the damage wrought by the previous ANC administration, led by Jacob Zuma, seemed almost quaint by comparison.

In the lead-up to the 2024 national and provincial elections, public debate became increasingly rancorous as South African voters lamented their decision in 2019 to open the door to a coalition government. Disaffected by the arrogance and corruption of the Zuma years, millions of voters had hoped that if the ANC got less than 50 per cent, spending five years in the cold while South Africa was governed by a national coalition formed by previous opposition parties would be a hard lesson in accountability that would force the ANC to mend its ways. But voters who thought that any coalition government would automatically exclude the ANC were grievously mistaken.

The acrimonious build-up to the 2024 election contrasted sharply with the euphoria that had erupted across urban South Africa five years earlier when the IEC announced that the ANC had failed to get a 50 per cent majority. There were all-night street parties in Gauteng and the Western Cape as the middle classes celebrated the fall of the liberators-turned-looters.

Voters widely assumed that the DA, EFF, and a number of smaller parties, including a new ANC alliance breakaway group, would form a new national government and provincial governments, at least in Gauteng. After all, both the DA and EFF had built their brands around opposing the Zuma-led ANC, and in March 2017, an EFF spokesperson had publicly stated that Julius Malema had no ambitions of returning to the ANC.[1] Multiparty metro coalitions also appeared to be going well in Nelson Mandela Bay, Johannesburg and Tshwane, where both DA and EFF voters were surprisingly quick to accept inter-party co-operation.

With the ANC vote having dropped below 50 per cent, it seemed logical for the DA and EFF – with support from smaller parties like the ACDP, FF+, COPE, UDM and IFP – to form a governing coalition. But the ANC and EFF had other ideas.

Playing the long game

Only a day after the final election results were announced, media reports began to surface about a meeting between Malema and a senior ANC delegation to discuss a coalition. In its all-consuming desire to remain in power, the ANC was apparently willing to forgive all the insults and invective the EFF had hurled at it over the years. No one was more shocked by this than the DA's leaders, who frantically tried to get in touch with their EFF counterparts. When the DA and EFF eventually met, Malema made it clear that his mind was made up, and that the meeting with the DA was simply a means of forcing greater concessions from the ANC.

The DA went into damage control mode. It accused the EFF of selling out millions of citizens who had voted to remove the ANC from power, and of being complicit in returning an illegitimate government to power. Many EFF voters agreed, and took to the streets in party strongholds like Rustenburg and Pretoria, demanding a halt to the negotiations with the ANC. But it was too late. It slowly dawned on EFF voters that this had been Malema's plan all along, and that they had been pawns in his grand political scheme.

As it became increasingly clear that South Africa (and Gauteng) would be governed by an ANC-EFF coalition, analysts rushed to say that it had been obvious all along that Malema's battle with Jacob Zuma was just a personal spat. With the benefit of perfect hindsight, they argued that the formation of the EFF had been a bargaining chip in a much longer game. Malema had created the EFF as a means of manipulating the ANC, and it had worked. The EFF had indeed played a decisive role in reducing the ANC vote to below 50 per cent. With Zuma gone, the path was now clear for Malema to return to the Ramaphosa-led ANC and claim his spoils. Desperate to hang on to power, the ANC acquiesced. The stage was set for Malema's triumphant – and toxic – homecoming.

The ANC, which was woefully unprepared for coalition negotiations and still reeling from the shock of losing the elections, capitulated to most of the EFF's demands. During the negotiations over cabinet portfolios, the ANC was only too happy to give the

EFF what it wanted. Besides Malema becoming deputy president, the ANC agreed that the EFF would control mining, agriculture, trade and industry, land reform, economic development, state security, justice, higher education, and communications. This gave the EFF near total control of the most productive economic sectors, and allowed it to exert political control by planting spies in the state security and justice ministries, and propagandists in the higher education and communications ministries.

The ANC and EFF agreed that deputy ministers would be drawn from the same parties as ministers. The ANC also agreed not to 'interfere' in ministries that 'belonged' to the EFF. The agreement effectively turned each ministry into the fiefdom of the party that controlled it, opening a path to unfettered patronage. The stipulation against 'interference' was written up in a flimsy one-page coalition agreement. Aside from committing both partners to 'radical economic transformation to emancipate the ethnic majority', the document did not specify any values that would guide the government's work, and did not even mention the Constitution. It also contained no guidelines for resolving disputes between the two parties, including at cabinet meetings.

After only three weeks of superficial negotiations that saw the ANC capitulate in the face of the EFF's tactics, the alliance was sworn into office. Malema's EFF rebels had returned home in a much stronger position than ever before. The negotiations made it obvious that the ANC was desperate to hang on to its patronage networks at any cost. While the ANC was nominally the senior partner in the relationship, the EFF held all the cards. As President Cyril Ramaphosa and Deputy President Malema moved into the Union Buildings, South Africans braced themselves for a devastating populist onslaught.

Crippling the state

The first blow came when the new administration affirmed its commitment to cadre deployment. The ANC had spent decades meticulously shoring up its support via a vast network of patronage, with cadre deployment – appointing senior public servants on the basis of loyalty to the party rather than competence – at its centre. The party was not about to undo a quarter century's worth of work, and risk losing control of key institutions to public-minded bureaucrats. More importantly, forsaking cadre deployment to build a meritocratic public service would eliminate the opportunities for ANC politicians to become instant millionaires through the control of government tenders and contracts. Amid a general feeding frenzy, they were not about to walk away from the trough.

As an offspring of the ANC, the EFF had a keen understanding of the centrality of corruption and cadre deployment in the ANC universe. (Prior to forming the EFF in 2013, Malema and his deputy, Floyd Shivambu, were respectively president and spokesperson for the ANC Youth League until they were both expelled for ill discipline in 2012). EFF leaders understood that, even if they wanted to challenge cadre deployment, they would run into a brick wall. But the EFF's betrayal of their campaign commitment to build a competent civil service went further than a mere inability to challenge the ANC's entrenched corruption culture.

Far from safeguarding public resources against political pillaging, the EFF soon joined the ANC in looting the state. Malema was of course no stranger to corruption allegations. In 2015, he was hit with 55 charges of fraud, racketeering, money laundering and corruption in connection with a R52 million tender granted to his company, On Point Engineering, by the Limpopo provincial government.[2] In a separate case, he was also accused of tax evasion to the tune of more than R16 million.[3]

These colours re-emerged once the EFF got its hands on power. The party emulated the ANC in selecting political apparatchiks to lead key public institutions. Both parties were aided in their pursuit of corruption by the fact that there was no joint oversight over their respective ministries. For example, with the EFF 'owning' the communications ministry, the ANC was powerless to oppose the appointment of an EFF propagandist as chief government spokesperson. Similarly, the EFF was perfectly content when the ANC continued its long-established practice of appointing a political hack who knew nothing about policing to lead the police service. The deal was simple: as long as the ANC left the EFF alone to build its own patronage network in the ministries under its control, the ANC could safely continue running its own rackets.

The co-option of the EFF also meant that the state had to create even more cushy jobs to accommodate party loyalists. The number of civil servants on the government payroll consequently swelled from an already unsustainable 2.69 million in 2014 to more than 3.2 million by 2024. In 2017, the public sector wage bill comprised 36 per cent of the national budget; by 2024, this figure had grown to nearly 50 per cent. It was expensive to make the corruption circle bigger, and taxpayers were footing the bill.

By choosing corruption over competence, the coalition effectively turned a blind eye to the biggest crisis plaguing the South African state. If the civil service was on the edge of an abyss prior to the 2019 elections, the ANC-EFF alliance tipped it over the edge.

As the government shed any remaining pretence that public servants were meant to serve the public, the civil service was drained of its last remaining skills. Eager to secure their pensions before the entire house of cards came tumbling down, and unable to work in a corrupt setting, the last remaining qualified and diligent state employees resigned in droves. With both parties eager to feed, the coalition had turned the state into a mere extension of its political masters; the line between politics and government was completely erased.

The consequences were predictable. Service delivery deteriorated as more and more public money was siphoned off into private bank accounts. The Auditor-General revealed that the amount of public funds lost to 'irregular expenditure' had more than tripled from an already staggering R46 billion in 2017[4] to R120 billion in 2024. With the public service drained of skills and morale, home affairs took months and even years to issue identity cards and passports, while the revenue service failed to collect taxes. Highways broke up, and water pipelines failed. As the cancer of corruption spread throughout the body politic, bribery became a near-daily experience for ordinary citizens.

Health care and education

The two sectors most vital to the wellbeing of South Africans – health care and education – effectively collapsed. Under increasing pressure as public trust deteriorated, the government worked itself into a populist fervour, and the coalition hurriedly implemented the national health insurance scheme. Although the legislation purportedly extended health coverage to all citizens, more cadre deployment meant that service levels at public hospitals continued to deteriorate.

Egged on by the ideologues in the EFF, the government disregarded warnings from the private sector that rapid and thoughtless implementation of national health insurance would lead to the collapse of private hospitals. With no credible plans in place for improving state hospitals, and amidst a hostile anti-private sector atmosphere, thousands of South African doctors resigned and emigrated. The scheme succeeded in equalising health care – it was equally poor for all.

A similar story unfolded in the higher education arena, where the EFF demanded immediate free education for all students up to their bachelor's degree. The call for 'free and decolonised' education also went up from a reinvigorated Fallist movement, which saw an opportunity to benefit from the election of a populist coalition. While some in the ANC objected to the proposal for free education, including for those students of all races who could afford to pay, the lack of a clear dispute resolution mechanism and the fear that the EFF would collapse the coalition won the day. Without improving the state's capacity to administer funding through institutions such as NSFAS, and without creating a viable funding model, the unilateral announcement that undergraduate education would be free sent shock waves through the university community.

Without the funds generated by tuition fees, which usually accounted for about one third of total income, universities were thrown into a financial crisis. University management teams had no choice but to make drastic spending cuts, including to vital infrastructure maintenance and staff salaries. Like their medical counterparts, many skilled academics went overseas. Those who could not or would not emigrate moved into the burgeoning private higher education sector, where groups such as AfriForum had made big investments in private community universities. As with health care, university education was now nominally free, but at the cost of quality and capacity.

With the ANC still in power, and as beholden as ever to the demands of labour unions like SADTU, the government made no effort to reform the basic education system. Instead, it introduced yet another revamped curriculum with a focus on 'patriotic education'. With the ANC still reeling from its election shock, the move reflected the coalition's increasingly populist and authoritarian bent. 'Patriotic education' was nothing more than a cynical political ploy to indoctrinate the country's children against 'regime change'. Predictably, South Africa's slide in international education rankings continued. The decision to play politics with basic education also worsened unemployment, as even fewer children graduated from high school with the basic skills required for finding work in an increasingly competitive and technology-driven formal economy.

Chasing Zimbabwe

Shortly after the ANC-EFF coalition assumed office, South Africa was subjected to a serious bout of collective déjà vu. It was as if the clock had been turned back to the late 2000s, when Malema and his populist cohorts first rose to power in the ANC Youth League. Citizens recalled how, at the time, Malema had launched a crusade aimed at forcing the ANC to expropriate land and nationalise mines without compensating private owners. The ideological battle over expropriation and nationalisation raged within the ANC for more than five years, until Malema's expulsion in 2012.

Malema and his acolytes then took the battle outside the ANC when they formed the EFF in 2013. Expropriation and nationalisation without compensation became a central pillar of the EFF's election manifestos, while Malema also continued his habit of launching into race-mongering rants. But with the EFF's return to the ANC camp in 2019 (albeit under a new name), the battle over land and minerals also returned to the ANC. As in the late 2000s, EFF members publicly ramped up the pressure on the ANC to endorse nationalisation.

However, in contrast with 2012, the ANC could not afford to sideline Malema's red brigade because, without the EFF, the ANC would find itself on the opposition benches. Unlike the DA, which had been in opposition throughout its existence and insisted that coalitions be based on predefined agreements centred on constitutional values, the ANC was determined to hang on to power at any cost. Without a comprehensive coalition agreement that spelled out the basis for co-operation, the battle over expropriation became a free-for-all.

Terrified of losing its grip on power and patronage, and with support from the populists in the conservative wing of the party, the ANC eventually agreed to allow expropriation without compensation by the land reform and mineral resources ministries, both controlled by the EFF. It took a dozen years, but Malema had finally won the ideological battle. The EFF had transformed the ANC into a purely populist outfit.

The coalition cabinet duly endorsed the nationalisation policy, which specified that all land, including commercial farmland, customary land, residential areas, as well as mines would be expropriated without compensation, and revert to state ownership. In turn, the state would lease out farms, residential stands and mines to 'deserving' beneficiaries. This despite the fact that the nationalisation model had already failed everywhere it had been tried in Africa, from Mozambique to Tanzania and Zimbabwe. This at a time when most other African states were slowly moving in the opposite direction, that is to say towards private and individual ownership. South Africa's populist coalition was out of step with the times.

The proposed policy ran into a wall of opposition as business leaders, opposition parties, and some civil society organisations mounted a fight-back. The ANC-EFF coalition's biggest problem was that it only held 62 per cent of Parliamentary seats, and therefore lacked the two-thirds majority required to abolish the private property clause in the Constitution. Despite the EFF's constant efforts to persuade enough MPs to vote for the constitutional amendment, the country had effectively reached a stalemate over the right to private property. It would be up to voters to decide the issue during the 2024 election. In the meantime, the coalition established a state mining company and formally took ownership of communal lands in the former homelands, where the unassailable power of local chiefs as the proxies of the corrupt state was codified into law.

Open government hostility to private economic activity triggered capital flight. The investment strike that had begun under the Zuma administration turned into full-scale divestment under the ANC-EFF administration. The value of land, homes, and mines collapsed as owners rushed to sell their properties. Banks and other investment institutions lost billions as customers defaulted on their loans. Even without a formal constitutional amendment, South Africa was no longer a safe investment destination. The EFF and ANC's socialist dream seemed about to come true, and the writing was on the wall.

An economic death spiral

The coalition's inability and unwillingness to rein in public sector spending, as well as its destructive land and mining policies, sent the economy into a self-reinforcing tailspin. As the economy weakened, the government responded with yet more populist policy measures. As in Venezuela and Zimbabwe in recent years, South Africa entered a death spiral.

Undeterred by warnings from 'imperialist' organisations such as the World Bank and the International Monetary Fund (IMF), the coalition imposed a minimum wage of R12 500 a month in all sectors of the economy. This figure was politically powerful as it was the same minimum wage demanded in 2012 by striking workers at Lonmin platinum mine at Marikana in North West, which resulted in 34 miners being killed by police. In anticipation of resistance from employers, the government also tightened the labour laws to make it even more difficult to fire redundant workers. The combination of an unaffordable minimum wage and rigid labour laws trapped many businesses between a rock and a hard place. While a few big companies had enough cash reserves to absorb the immediate impact, hundreds of small- and medium-sized firms had no choice but to close their doors.

The government complemented these efforts by imposing increasingly arduous BEE requirements for private companies. The new regulations required all domestic firms to be at least

80 per cent black-owned in order to reflect national demographics, while foreign companies were forced to sell their shares to domestic 'empowerment partners'. The greatest beneficiaries of the scheme were well-connected ANC/EFF elites, who gleefully took majority ownership of companies formerly managed by 'white monopoly capital'. But it was a hollow victory. By the time the illegal seizure of wealth was complete, many of the shares were not worth the paper they were printed on.

As Eskom followed other SOEs down the drain, rolling blackouts returned. The government used the power crisis as a fig-leaf to give final approval for a nuclear power deal with Russia at a cost of more than R1 trillion.[5] The coalition fulfilled another long-standing populist ambition by imposing massive import tariffs that isolated South Africa from the global trading system. Without adequate capacity to manufacture substitutes for products that were formerly imported, the country soon experienced shortages of everything from new vehicles to toilet paper. The World Trade Organization (WTO) sanctioned the country for breaking trade rules, while important trading partners such as the European Union retaliated by imposing its own tariffs on South African imports.

As access to capital dried up, the coalition created a state bank, and forced commercial banks to dole out increasingly risky loans to customers with poor credit scores. The ANC-EFF administration further nationalised the Reserve Bank, and changed its mandate to bring it under the control of the executive. As economic conditions worsened, the Reserve Bank was strong-armed into printing money. Inflation started rising, reaching 60 per cent by 2024.

Democracy under siege

Many South Africans refused to accept this plunge into disaster. In urban centres, voters rebelled during the 2021 municipal elections, making the DA the largest party in six out of the country's eight metros. However, after DA-led coalitions had assumed control of the cities, the national ANC-EFF alliance turned to an old trick to suppress the rise of opposition coalitions at the municipal level.

Back in 2006, the ANC's Richard Dyantyi had threatened to collapse the DA-led coalition in Cape Town by changing the structure of the city's mayoral committee, thereby robbing the coalition of its majority.[6] In 2017, the ANC similarly threatened to usurp power in Nelson Mandela Bay when it instructed the provincial government to put the municipality 'under administration,'[7] thereby robbing the opposition coalition of its ability to manage the metro.

While the earlier threats did not materialise, by the early 2020s, the ANC-EFF coalition no longer had any qualms about grabbing power from subnational governments. It regularly manufactured reasons to put municipalities under administration, undermining the ability of its opponents to implement an alternative to the populist agenda.

During the first two years of the national ANC-EFF alliance, hundreds of thousands of citizens flooded the streets to protest against the government's continued corruption and economic malfeasance. Emboldened by the fact that the once invincible ANC's voting share had dropped below 50 per cent in the 2019 election, many protesters believed that the country's democracy was strong enough to force the government out of office, and trigger fresh elections. They pointed to the constitutional protection of free speech and peaceful protest, as well as a largely independent media and judiciary, as evidence that the country remained a vibrant democracy.

Media capture

But the space for freedom and independence from government *diktat* was shrinking. For one, the media was rapidly being co-opted into the populist project. Like so many of the country's afflictions, media capture dated back to the Zuma years when, in 2010, the Gupta family founded the pro-Zuma newspaper *The New Age*. In 2013, the Zuma administration also funnelled public money to the ANC sycophant Iqbal Survé to help him take over and partially transform the ironically named Independent Newspaper Group into an ANC mouthpiece. As allegations of corruption and state capture mounted, the next step in the shrinking of media independence came with the Gupta family's founding of the ANN7 television station, also in 2013.

Many sober-minded citizens initially laughed off the Gupta media empire as a blatant propaganda vehicle designed to shield the ruling clique from justice. The ANN7 channel, broadcast 24 hours a day on the DStv satellite network, became a laughing stock for its amateurish lack of the most basic journalistic skills. But, as the years went by, ANN7 eliminated some of the most glaring errors, and fine-tuned its propaganda techniques. As public pressure mounted on Jacob Zuma to resign over his links with the Guptas, the channel continued to air around-the-clock programming aimed at discrediting Zuma's opponents.

Media outlets aligned to the ANC, including *The New Age*, ANN7 and Independent Newspapers, also diligently watered the seeds of populism and racial scapegoating. These outlets parroted the narratives of 'radical economic transformation' and 'white monopoly capital', slogans that were purposefully designed by the British public relations agency, Bell Pottinger, to deflect attention away from the ANC's crimes. By the time the 2019 election rolled around, significant parts of the country's media landscape were already infected with populist sentiments.

As the post-2019 ANC-EFF coalition intensified its onslaught against the economy, these captured media houses employed the same tactics they had originally used to defend Zuma and the Guptas. The difference was that, over the years, they had got vastly better at it. While the early days of captured media were characterised by incompetent and clumsy attempts to flood social media platforms with fake bots, and society with fake news, by the early 2020s, media propagandists had honed their craft. The country's press was decidedly less free than a decade earlier, and it was littered with outright hatred directed at white people and other ethnic minorities.

Judiciary undermined

The judiciary was also not immune to the populist disease. As street protests and corruption allegations mounted, the coalition dug in its heels. Under the guise of defeating 'reactionary' judges, the executive increasingly disregarded the recommendations of the judicial service commission. Instead, they chose to appoint judges who were sympathetic to the populist ideological project. Brave judges who continued to uphold the rule of law in the face of ideological pressure were labelled as sell-outs or defenders of 'white monopoly capital', and put under pressure to resign.

No longer free

By the end of the government's term in mid-2024, the ANC-EFF alliance had spread its tentacles throughout all sectors of society. An intensified version of the decades-old cadre deployment policy was the primary tool in this process, as it allowed the populist government not only to exert control over the top echelons of the state, but also to increasingly control what was left of the economy. Every industry that was nationalised or suffocated into compliance gave the populists another lever of social control.

Everything from land holdings to minerals and the financial sector were either already under state control, or under severe threat. There were very few private companies left that could make business decisions without explicit approval from some state agency. Acts of bribery and corruption soared, as the government used its control to extract patronage at every turn. The model of cadre deployment that had worked so well in giving the ANC complete control over nominally independent state institutions proved equally as effective in establishing control over the 'commanding heights' of the economy.

Building on the solid foundation that the ANC had constructed in the preceding decades, the populist forces unleashed by the ANC-EFF coalition needed only five short years to tame a media corps that had once been fiercely independent. The alliance's ideology of total control also enabled it to neuter a judiciary that used to be admired the world over for its fearlessness in the face of power abuse. Equally, as many business people divested and emigrated, South Africa's few remaining industries operated almost entirely at the mercy of the new oligarchs.

The initial optimism that the constitutionally protected right to public protest would be enough to reign in the populist excesses proved misplaced. While protest was still tolerated during its first two years in power, the coalition became more repressive as resistance mounted. In the lead-up to the 2024 election campaign, South Africans faced the sombre possibility that the era of free and fair elections could be over.

A dead end

The roots of South Africa's populist turn lay in the ANC's determination to hang on to power at any cost. By the time it assumed power in 1994, the ANC had convinced itself that it was the only political vehicle capable of representing the wishes and aspirations of the country's black majority. During the first two-and-a-half decades of democracy, this attitude of entitlement was reinforced by each successive election, in which the party would invariably end up with an overwhelming majority. Except for the Western Cape, the ANC never had to face the possibility of losing its grip on power.

Despite the many warning signs that preceded it, the 2019 election loss thus came as a debilitating shock to the party. For the first time since its founding more than a century earlier, the ANC had to consider the possibility that it no longer held a monopoly on political legitimacy, as more than half of South African voters had rejected it. But instead of facing up to their fallibility, party leaders were desperate to retain control over the national government (and Gauteng). After all, it is impossible to dole out government contracts to party cronies from the opposition benches.

The ANC had to find a way of enticing the EFF away from forming a coalition with the DA. The key difference between the ANC and DA was that the ANC had never been in opposition, while the DA was used to it. This meant that the DA had a clear bottom line in its negotiations with the EFF, because the party knew it would survive another five years in opposition. In contrast, the panicked ANC was willing to write a blank cheque in exchange for the EFF's co-operation. Its blind lust for power at any cost meant that it ultimately conceded to almost every EFF demand, because the alternative – being in opposition – was too ghastly to contemplate for a party that believed it had the right to rule 'forever . . . until Jesus comes back'.[8]

Debt crisis

The populist coalition's spending spree triggered an unprecedented debt crisis. By 2024, the country's public debt had outstripped its annual GDP. Inflation was at an all-time high, and although the government took to manipulating the data, figures showed that the official unemployment rate had increased to at least 35 per cent, while the expanded unemployment rate stood at over 50 per cent. As desperation spread, violent crime escalated to warlike levels.

The recession that had hit South Africa in 2017 proved to be only a foretaste of what was to come. By 2024, the country was trapped in a full-scale depression as the economy shrunk by 1.5 per cent a year. The average citizen was significantly worse off, as GDP per capita had plunged from $12 260 in 2016[9] to $8 000 in 2024. Perversely, the government nonetheless claimed credit for reducing the country's Gini inequality score from 0.63 to 0.55, as poverty became more equally distributed throughout society.

In contrast to the optimism that had characterised election day in 2019, South Africans were deeply disillusioned as they headed

148

to the polls five years later. As the populist coalition intensified its scapegoating of minorities in order to mask its own failures, racial discrimination against white, coloured and Indian people was a daily reality. Just as in the late 1980s, the air was full of talk that the country was headed for some kind of racial war.

A costly miscalculation

Many voters had believed that dragging the ANC below 50 per cent in 2019 would trigger an era of political and economic renewal under an opposition coalition government that would bring out the best in the DA and EFF. However, most voters underestimated the possibility that the prospect of losing power would bring out the worst in the ANC. Even fewer people expected that the EFF would so easily betray its staunchly anti-ANC rhetoric to form an alliance with the party it professed to despise. In their unprincipled pursuit of power, the ANC and EFF had built a relationship which simply deepened corruption, and strengthened the hand of populists and racial ideologues.

The country was on a path to disaster. As propaganda filled the air, and dejected voters went to the polls, many doubted that the election would be legitimate. Nevertheless, the election provided what was perhaps the final opportunity for South Africans to stop the bleeding. If enough voters turned on the ANC-EFF alliance, there was a chance that their combined total would drop below 50 per cent. Whatever the outcome, South Africans now fully understood the strategic importance of their vote. Above all, they also grasped that the future of the country depended on which configuration of political parties could cobble together the next governing coalition.

Chapter Seven

Going nowhere slowly

It's the year 2024, and South Africa is governed by a DA-led minority government. However, while the DA is nominally in charge, it needs to negotiate support in Parliament for every piece of legislation it wants to implement. This means that governance is a very slow process. The DA-led government has managed to reduce corruption and maladministration, and introduce some meaningful economic and social reforms. But voters are hoping that, following the forthcoming national and provincial elections, in which no party is again likely to gain an absolute majority, leaders will be willing to do the work needed to build workable and lasting governing coalitions.

Looking back from 2024, most South Africans were more cynical than ever about the country's politics. In the lead-up to the 2019 elections, analysts and opposition leaders had boldly predicted that once the ANC vote fell below 50 per cent, South Africa would enter a promising new era of coalition politics. Disgruntled by decades of misrule, and excited by the prospect of a new governing coalition, millions of urbanites turned their backs on the ANC. When the IEC announced that no single political party had garnered 50 per cent majorities at the national level or in Gauteng, residents of most major towns and cities looked forward to a fundamental shift in how the country was managed.

The public was whipped into a frenzy of speculation over which groups would partner up to form a government. Most people argued that a DA-EFF coalition which also included smaller parties and an ANC splinter group was the most logical outcome, given that all opposition parties had vigorously campaigned against the ANC. Others felt that the EFF would seize upon the opportunity to rejoin the ANC, with the aim of finally implementing the populist policies it had long agitated for. One thing that both camps agreed on was that great change was on the horizon. All these predictions turned out to be wrong.

No compromise

Following the election, political parties had 30 days to cobble together a majority in Parliament to elect the country's next president, who would then appoint her or his cabinet. The media initially reported that the EFF was likely to partner with the DA, but as negotiations dragged into a second week, it seemed likely that the EFF would go with the ANC. The press was rife with misinformation as party insiders tried to bend the public narrative in their favour. The public revelled in the drama, delighted to see competitive democracy in action after 25 years of one-party hegemony.

However, as inter-party negotiations entered its third week, the atmosphere changed. Exhausted by the constant media speculation, people became concerned about the apparent lack of progress. Two days before the 30-day deadline, the chief justice (who was charged with overseeing the election of the president) finally announced that Parliament would hold its first sitting. With only one day to spare, the 400 members of the National Assembly convened in Cape Town.

With no obvious resolution in sight after a month of non-stop speculation, South Africans tuned into the proceedings in Parliament under an atmosphere akin to a rugby World Cup final. After the chief justice had dispensed with the formalities, he announced that the first item on the agenda was the election of a new Parliamentary speaker. In a sign that a strategy did indeed exist, both the ANC and EFF nominated a candidate for speaker, but the DA did not nominate anyone. Social media erupted in a flurry of conjecture about the DA's choice. After the votes were tallied, the EFF's candidate was supported by the DA, and emerged as the victor by a very narrow margin.

The move triggered a minor panic on Twitter, as users contemplated the one possibility they had not considered: that South Africa was about to get an EFF president. But the nominations for president revealed another twist in the tale. The ANC again nominated its candidate, Cyril Ramaphosa, while the DA nominated its leader, Mmusi Maimane. This time, the EFF did not nominate anyone. Although the vote was conducted by secret ballot, it was clear that the EFF had decided to support the DA's candidate. By a margin of only two votes, Maimane was elected as president.

While the DA and EFF had agreed to support one another's candidates for speaker and president, they did not establish a formal governing coalition. Instead, South Africa now had a minority government. This meant that Maimane was free to appoint DA members to his cabinet, giving the party control over the executive (although the DA also invited a number of smaller parties, including the ACDP, COPE, IFP, FF+ and UDM, to join its cabinet). But this power would be checked by a deeply divided legislature, in which the EFF would direct the agenda.

The EFF's reasoning soon became clear. Although the party believed it could extract far bigger concessions from the ANC than from the DA, it concluded that its credibility would go up in smoke if it partnered with the ANC at a time when voters had rejected the latter party. While its voters would probably be more willing to stomach a coalition with the DA, EFF leaders reasoned that they would not be able to implement their agenda or build patronage networks in a partnership with the DA. As was the case in Johannesburg and Tshwane following the 2016 municipal elections, the EFF decided not to establish a formal coalition with either the DA or the ANC.

But the EFF still held the deciding vote in Parliament, which meant that it would have to support one of the two parties' candidates in the Parliamentary vote. If it refused to support either of the two, the country would have to hold fresh elections. Party leaders concluded that, if it was not worth the risk to support the ANC in a formal coalition in which they would at least be able to extract many concessions, it made even less sense to be seen as returning the ANC to power in a minority government where it would not be a formal partner.

Based on this process of elimination, the EFF figured that establishing a DA-led minority government would be its best bet. It reached the same conclusion in Gauteng. On the one hand, this would enable the EFF to claim that it upheld democracy by removing the ANC in accordance with voters' wishes. On the other, the party could argue that it was not complicit in the DA's agenda, while still holding the Maimane-led executive to account via its control of the Parliamentary speaker's seat. While the DA was nominally in charge, it needed to win support in Parliament for each and every piece of legislation it wanted to implement.

A rocky start

The DA minority administration's first challenge was to get a grip on the country's unsustainable debt levels by reining in public sector spending, and curbing corruption. It aimed to do this by undertaking a comprehensive review of the qualifications and skills of all civil servants, and subjecting all appointments to approval by the Public Service Commission. But to achieve this, the DA needed the legislature to pass a set of amendments to public administration legislation. The proposal immediately ran into fierce resistance from a hostile Parliament that was determined to stamp its authority on the DA government.

The attempt to clean up the state provided a foretaste of just how difficult it would be for the government to implement its agenda fully. Despite forming a coalition with a group of smaller parties, the DA was still well short of a 50 per cent majority in Parliament, which meant that it had to secure sufficient support from opposition parties in order to adopt the proposed new law. The ANC was unmoved. With thousands of its cronies still employed in powerful positions throughout the civil service, the ANC was determined to block any efforts that would see public servants lose their jobs. The cadre network it had put in place since 1994 allowed the ANC to retain control of many state departments, and cadres' fealty to the ANC could be a useful tool to undermine the new administration.

Given the ANC's refusal to co-operate, the DA turned to the EFF and other minor parties for support. Because they did not have any control over existing public service patronage networks, these parties were not fundamentally opposed to a reform process that would see the construction of a more capable state.

However, they revelled in their new-found ability to check and even block legislative action – something that had been nearly impossible during the 25 years of ANC domination.

With party discipline no longer sufficient to force legislation through Parliament, the DA undertook a series of negotiations with opposition lawmakers. Parliament was transformed from a sleepy retirement home where ANC legislators previously went to collect their pensions into a vibrant centre of political life. Media reports informed the public about non-stop, behind-the-scenes horse-trading as the DA sought to secure opposition support, while the ANC tried to undermine the negotiations. Party caucuses haggled over which negotiating position would play best with the public, and how to extract as many concessions as possible while still holding on to their manifesto promises.

While this was a welcome change from the stale atmosphere under one-party rule, the public soon became exasperated about the lack of progress. The DA's proposed amendments to the public administration law were ultimately stuck in Parliament for over a year. Alarmed by the lost time, the cabinet decided to explore an alternative approach. Using the significant powers bestowed on the president, the government enacted a raft of public administration changes that did not require Parliamentary approval. The cabinet used a combination of regulations, policies and presidential proclamations to get around the gridlock in Parliament. Instead of formally adopting a new law that would require civil servants to be tested and vetted, each national government department drew up a new set of executive regulations and policies that had a similar effect. The policies amounted to a watered-down version of what the legal amendments had sought to achieve.

Negotiations in Parliament only began moving again after opposition parties saw that the executive would try to circumvent their resistance. The legal amendments that were ultimately adopted vividly reflected the many months of horse-trading that went into their drafting. For instance, in order to soften the ANC's resistance, the law included provisions that the government would do its best to find other jobs for (ANC-aligned) state employees who did not have the requisite qualifications to stay on in senior positions. In a concession to the EFF, the amendments also prohibited the use of labour brokers in the hiring of junior and temporary state employees.

After more than two years of haggling, the DA-led minority government had only made limited progress. It was unable to remove many unqualified officials, and failed to give the Public Service Commission near-total powers over appointments. Nonetheless, the policy changes and limited Parliamentary amendments meant that the number of state employees had been reduced from 2.69 million in 2014 to 2.3 million in 2024. However, the public sector wage bill had only declined slightly from 36 per cent of the national budget to 34 per cent.

The government's efforts to reform the education and health care sectors followed a similarly mixed pattern. The DA used its executive control over the education and health departments to introduce stricter management controls over teachers and health workers. But the government failed to get its way when changes required legislative amendments – such as the DA's plan to bar senior education officials who were not teachers from being SADTU members. The ANC naturally refused to co-operate, given its hold over the teachers' union. At the same time, other opposition parties adopted an obstructionist posture or tried to extract as many concessions as possible from the DA in exchange for their support. Although financial audits and media reports revealed halting progress, it was not enough to reverse the collapse in public service delivery.

Running in one place

As ordinary South Africans and their elected lawmakers got used to the partisan gridlock and horse-trading inherent to minority governance, opposition parties grew increasingly confident in their ability to control the political agenda even though they did not occupy the Union Buildings. About one year after the DA had occupied the seat of government, the ANC and EFF illustrated how a keen understanding of the rules of Parliament could empower opposition parties to strongly influence the political narrative in a divided government.

It started when the EFF introduced new legislation as a private member's bill to the Parliamentary committee on land reform. In line with the EFF's long-standing call for the expropriation of 'white-owned land', the bill proposed that the government should expropriate all commercial farmland and mines without compensation. (The proposal cleverly stopped short of calling for a constitutional amendment to remove the right to private property, as this would have required a two-thirds majority rather than a simple majority.) Empowering the government to expropriate property without compensation was sure to devastate the economy, and the DA naturally opposed the bill during committee hearings.

However, despite being in government, the DA did not control a coalition with a majority of Parliamentary seats. In a shock development, ANC and EFF members of the land reform committee voted together in support of the amendment. The EFF-aligned speaker of Parliament quickly scheduled a debate on the matter in the National Assembly. After a vigorous debate, the legislation was passed by a slim margin, supported by EFF and ANC MPs. The law, which violated all the DA's political and economic principles, ended up on President Maimane's desk for his signature.

According to the Constitution, the president either had to assent to the law, or refer it back to Parliament if he felt it did not pass constitutional muster. In the case of the expropriation law, Maimane argued that even though the law was couched in different terms, it violated the constitutional right to private property. He duly returned the bill to the National Assembly for reconsideration. But the EFF and ANC were delighted by the publicity they were getting, and refused to budge.

In another political ploy, the ANC called for a motion of no confidence in the DA administration over Maimane's refusal to sign the expropriation bill into law. Both the ANC and EFF backed the motion in Parliament, and just like that, South Africa's government came tumbling down. It was an unprecedented crisis, and members of the public were furious, with protests erupting across the country. The National Assembly again had 30 days to elect a new president. Shaken by the public's anger at its decision to vote with the ANC, the EFF again agreed to support the DA, and effectively re-establish the minority government. At the end of the most chaotic and bizarre month in the country's democratic history, the DA-led minority administration was back in office. The EFF claimed the whole episode was intended to 'teach the DA a lesson'.

As if nothing had happened, Parliament again passed the expropriation bill by a slim margin, and sent it back to Maimane as soon as he was back in office. The Constitution was clear on what should happen next. If, after reconsideration, the bill still did not accommodate the president's reservations, (s)he must 'refer it to the Constitutional Court for a decision on its constitutionality. If the Constitutional Court decides that the bill is constitutional, the president must assent to and sign it.'[1]

Maimane consequently sent the bill to the Constitutional Court which, after months of proceedings, agreed that the law violated section 25 of the county's fundamental law. The court advised that MPs who were in favour of the law needed to follow the correct channels if they wanted a constitutional amendment. But the EFF and ANC did not control the requisite two-thirds majority of seats in Parliament, which precluded them from amending the Constitution.

The court's ruling came more than three years into the minority government's term. Although the proposed legislation was ultimately struck down, it had severely damaged the country's international reputation. Investment in agriculture and mining continued to decline as farmers sold their land, and mining companies packed up and left. The legal uncertainty generated by the spectacle of the no-confidence motion also significantly slowed down the DA government's own efforts to speed up land reform.

With the opposition proposal finally defeated, the government managed to engineer greater progress in other social areas. In fact, in sectors like housing, the DA was able to implement significant parts of its agenda, because it did not need to strike compromises with any formal coalition partners. Over time, the government's emphasis shifted away from only building RDP houses towards more market-based solutions. The DA government lifted the ban on the sale of RDP houses for a period of eight years after being handed to a beneficiary, and abolished transfer duties for first-time buyers of homes costing less than R2 million. The cabinet also resolved to improve South Africa's *Doing Business* ranking, among others by simplifying the process of surveying and registering property. In 2017, it took an average of 23 days to register a property bond.[2] By 2024, the processing time was reduced to only seven days.

Towards the end of its term, in the wake of the time lost to the expropriation bill and no-confidence fiasco, the DA revealed an ambitious plan to speed up land reform by surveying and titling all land parcels in the former homelands. But the ANC and EFF blocked the proposal in Parliament. Although the DA had reduced corruption in the land redistribution process – and despite the political fireworks that surrounded it – the result of political bickering between the executive and legislature was that the policy framework for land reform had changed very little during the minority government's five-year term. The 16 million residents of the former homelands still lacked legal rights to their land, and land redistribution continued to be slow and inefficient. With two vastly different proposals from the ANC/EFF and the DA on the table, it would be up to voters to resolve the impasse in the 2024 election.

Two steps forward, one step back

In the face of legislative opposition, the minority government decided to exploit every last ounce of its executive power. Hiring

good legal advisers became a priority for all government departments, as ministers looked for ways to enact policy changes
that did not require Parliamentary approval. While fundamental
changes to health care, education, land reform and other social
sectors were very difficult to enact without a Parliamentary
majority, the Constitution bestowed much greater powers on the
executive to determine economic and foreign policy.

The DA was thus able to implement many of the economic
reforms it had promised voters in the 2019 campaign. It also
pushed to remake South Africa's international image. In contrast
to the Zuma era, when the government was hostile to liberal-
democratic norms such as the rule of law and protecting universal human rights, the Maimane administration internalised those
values. It launched a thorough investigation into the failure to
arrest the Sudanese war criminal Omar Al-Bashir during a visit to
South Africa,[3] as well as the decision to grant diplomatic immunity to former Zimbabwean first lady Grace Mugabe after she had
assaulted a young woman in Johannesburg in 2017.[4] South Africa's voting behaviour at the United Nations also changed substantially, as the country joined the ranks of other liberal
societies in putting pressure on authoritarian regimes from
Russia to Cuba. After the damage done to the country's reputation by the corruption under the ANC, the DA government's commitment to liberal values slowly restored South Africa's standing
in the free world.

Back home, the government focused on the energy sector. It
scrapped its predecessor's plans to build nuclear energy, and
overhauled the country's integrated resources plan. Instead of
adopting unaffordable nuclear energy in the midst of a lingering

debt crisis, the administration opened up the energy market to independent power producers. The new energy regulations also actively promoted investment in renewable sources such as wind and solar power. By 2024, more than 15 per cent of the country's electricity came from renewable sources, up from just 4.5 per cent in 2016.[5] The shift broke Eskom's monopoly on electricity generation, as it opened the sector to competition from private firms. The new regulations also weakened Eskom's hold over electricity transmission by allowing independent power producers to feed electricity directly into the national power grid.

Despite noisy opposition from the ANC and EFF, the public enterprises ministry used its considerable power to reform the country's 717 SOEs. Throughout its two decades in opposition, the DA had consistently criticised the way in which the ANC allowed failing public entities to drag down South Africa's economy. With at least one hand finally on the steering wheel, the DA was determined to effect sweeping changes. As a first step, it launched a comprehensive review of all SOEs in order to determine which assets could become productive and profitable, and which should be sold.

Once the review report was complete, the government acted. It sold off large parts of failing enterprises like SAA. In other cases, such as Transnet, it pursued partial privatisation while retaining a majority stake. While each entity was judged according to its own particular situation, the government used its powers of appointment to get rid of ANC cadres and put in place competent senior managers for all public enterprises. The rationalisation of SOEs injected welcome cash into the government coffers. Even though much of the money went to repaying government debt, the administration used the remainder to fund upgrades to railways, roads, ports and internet infrastructure.

But the minority administration ran into far greater difficulties when it tried to adjust labour policies to stimulate employment growth. In contrast to the economic sphere, where the executive had a lot of policy-making leeway, the DA needed legislative support from other parties to change the labour laws. In a series of Parliamentary meetings, the governing party argued in favour of greater labour flexibility. Specifically, the DA wanted to repeal section 32 of the Labour Relations Act, which extended wage agreements across entire sectors and therefore disadvantaged small businesses that were unable to absorb the higher costs. It similarly wanted to repeal sections 18 and 26 of the act that entrenched the dominance of big unions over entire sectors.[6] The DA also proposed to exempt businesses that employed fewer than 250 workers from onerous administrative requirements in the act, and make it easier for small businesses to hire and fire workers.

But the party's proposals were anathema to both the ANC (because of its cosy relationship with organised labour) and the EFF (because of its anti-private sector ideology). The proposed amendments were bogged down for months as Parliamentary leaders negotiated behind the scenes. A minor breakthrough eventually came when the EFF announced that it would support the amendments aimed at curbing the power of dominant unions and changing the definition of 'big employer' to companies with more than 250 workers. In exchange, the DA agreed to ban labour brokers in the platinum industry. The legislation was ultimately passed with support from the DA and EFF.

The inclusion of such a seemingly random provision into the labour law constituted the first example in South Africa of what is termed 'pork-barrel politics' in the United States. In order to get buy-in from the EFF for this particular piece of legislation, the DA included an unrelated provision that would directly benefit mine workers in the North West's platinum belt – a key EFF constituency. As political parties got used to the gridlock and trade-offs inherent to minority government, pork-barrel politics became an increasingly common feature of law-making.

Breakup

The election of an executive that did not control a majority of seats in Parliament entrenched divisions within South African society. On the one hand, the minority government partially succeeded in enacting productive economic reforms. The opening up of energy and other markets through the partial privatisation of former state monopolies created a host of new business opportunities for entrepreneurs. Those who had gone to good schools and had access to capital set up new businesses that began to prosper, while delivering higher quality services to its customers. This new class of entrepreneurs was supported by a more business-friendly policy framework and a government committed to the rule of law and the independence of institutions like the Reserve Bank.

But the DA's lack of a Parliamentary majority hampered its ability to implement the more fundamental reforms that could only come through legislative changes. Under a formal coalition, the key challenge was to get coalition partner(s) to agree on any given policy change. Once an internal agreement was in place, the coalition's built-in legislative majority meant that most of its proposals would be adopted into law without much difficulty. Since the DA minority government lacked a formal coalition partner, it had no built-in majority. Instead of only hashing out differences with one or two coalition partners, it had to negotiate with all opposition parties represented in Parliament on an issue-by-issue basis.

This massively slowed down the law-making process. As was potently illustrated in the fight over land reform legislation, it also meant that opposition parties could block and even override the government's intended policies. Despite some exceptions, such as the halting changes to labour laws, the effect was largely to maintain the status quo. While the minority government was able to make progress in areas where it had significant discretionary powers – such as determining economic and foreign policy – it was unable to bring about real change in areas that required formal legislative amendments, such as land, education, health care, and civil service reform.

This resulted in higher levels of social and economic inequality. People who had the requisite skills saw real benefits from a freer, more competitive and more market-friendly economy. But those without skills and capital fell even further behind, as the deadlock in Parliament meant that nothing was really done to improve public schooling and health care. In other words, based on the South African legal framework, the minority government had the power to address weaknesses on the demand-side of the economy, but it did not have the same ability to launch supply-side interventions without support from a co-operative Parliament. South Africa desperately needed both types of reforms, but the minority administration was only able to address one side of the coin.

The minority government's term of office intensified many trends that had emerged during the preceding decades. Highly skilled workers and business people continued to prosper, while the poor largely remained locked out. Regional economies boomed in urban areas of the country where many high skilled workers clustered together, but rural areas sank ever deeper into poverty. While urban policing improved due to somewhat better management, rural crime rates, including brutal farm murders, continued to climb. Social inequalities worsened, as the wealthy retreated even deeper into security complexes and other enclaves.

A short fuse

By the end of the administration's term, voters looked back at the previous five years with mixed emotions. Very few had expected that South Africa would end up with a minority government after the ANC fell. When the ANC lost its dominant majority in 2019, most observers predicted that the country was on the cusp of great change. Instead, the inability of political parties to form a coalition that commanded a Parliamentary majority revealed how ossified and divided South African politics still was. Far from overcoming their differences, and hammering out a progressive coalition compromise in the interest of voters, political leaders dug in their heels and refused to co-operate formally.

But not choosing is also a choice. By opting for a minority government over a majority coalition, MPs essentially elected to retain the social status quo while allowing the executive to tinker around the economic edges. The minority cabinet did not have the mandate, legitimacy or majority to truly turn the country around. The numbers told the story. Between 2019 and 2024, the economy grew at an annual average of 2.8 per cent – better than during the Zuma years, but still well below the country's potential.

Even though GDP per capita increased from $12 260 in 2016[7] to $14 000 in 2024, poverty only decreased marginally. The *Doing Business* index showed that it was now much easier to conduct business in the country, but the official unemployment rate remained steady at 25 per cent. Moreover, as the rich disproportionately reaped the benefits of a liberalised economy while the poor largely remained locked out, the Gini score for inequality increased from 0.63 to 0.68 under the divided government.

At the top of the income pyramid, a multiracial urban elite praised the changes brought about by the minority government. From its vantage point, the DA administration had reduced corruption and maladministration while enacting sensible economic policies that had saved the country from the destructive populist path embarked upon by the Zuma administration. The economic elite often spoke about how they felt a renewed sense of pride in being South African when travelling abroad. The democratic world indeed heaped praise on the country for turning away from the ANC's increasingly populist demagoguery. International media lauded South Africa as a country with a consolidated democracy that was moving in the right direction, while much of the world was sliding towards authoritarianism.

But the improvements engineered by the minority government were only part of the story, and in many ways only skin-deep. Although the administration had halted the slide towards a failed state, the lives of many citizens – especially the rural poor – did not improve. Far too many people were still jobless. Many schools and hospitals were in bad shape, as the government tried to fix problems with one hand tied behind its back.

Nevertheless, in the run-up to the 2024 polls, most citizens were relieved that the ship of state was steadier than five years earlier. Having lived through a peaceful transfer of power, few feared that the country was about to turn into the next Zimbabwe or Venezuela. But there was a sense that while the time bomb had been reset, it had not been defused. Many voters understood that the root of the problem lay in the refusal of political parties to compromise and form a formal coalition government that had the legitimacy and majority required to enact more fundamental change. It was again likely that no single party would garner a 50 per cent majority in 2024. Voters hoped that, this time around, political leaders would be willing to do the hard work needed to build workable coalitions, rather than opting for the path of least resistance.

PART THREE

Preparing for plurality

Chapter Eight

The Government of National Unity

The three scenarios of coalition governments in South Africa, as well as the discussion of international experiences of coalition governments in Chapter Four, show clearly that the outcomes of coalition government are not predetermined. Some fail due to infighting, the pursuit of ruinous policies, or both. Others develop a firm basis for co-operation by fostering a culture of productive compromise, underpinned by clear procedures for settling disputes when (not *if*) they arise.

Thus far, we have addressed two questions: *why* coalitions are coming in South Africa, and *what* that could mean for the country. We now turn to the *how*: how to ensure that South Africa leverages coalitions to become an economically prosperous Germany (or even a relatively successful India), rather than a ruined Nepal.

The good news is that we have agency. The fact that coalitions can be good, bad or broken tells us that each society shapes the environment in which coalitions operate – to their advantage, or to their detriment. As the three scenarios have demonstrated, coalitions reserve a particularly important role for political leaders. In a one-party government, political leaders are largely assured of a Parliamentary majority, which makes it relatively easy to pass legislation. In a coalition government, the need to maintain a majority that depends on the co-operation of partners means that political leaders face a much bigger challenge: in order to get anything done, they need to manage relations with their partners constantly to keep the government together (or, under a minority government, continually build new legislative majorities). Once support for the ANC falls below 50 per cent, political leadership and the ability to manage coalitions will become the single most important requirement for progress.

But successful coalitions do not hinge on astute political leadership only. Just as important – and probably even more difficult to achieve – is the need for society at large to build and internalise a coalition culture. Even with competent political leaders, coalition governments can fail when the society in which they are embedded rejects compromise in favour of a zero-sum – usually racial or ethnic – approach to politics, in terms of which one party's victory is seen as another party's defeat.

Part Three addresses these issues. Although coalitions have not yet become the default mode of governance in South Africa, there have already been at least two instances where coalitions have worked well: the Government of National Unity (GNU) between 1994 and 1996, and the multiparty coalition that governed Cape Town between 2006 and 2011. Chapters Eight and Nine examine these two home-grown cases in order to identify some of the tools political leaders can use to strengthen coalition governments.

Chapter Ten draws lessons from the GNU and Cape Town stories, and uses these to develop concrete recommendations for how to make coalitions work. It also returns to the question of what society at large can do to build a coalition culture that provides political leaders with incentives to co-operate and govern in the interest of all citizens. Finally, based on the lessons distilled from the case studies, Chapter Eleven surveys the contemporary South African political landscape to see which of the three scenarios discussed previously are most likely to come to pass should ANC support fall below 50 per cent in the 2019 national elections.

No foregone conclusion

Chapter Four introduced the Government of National Unity (GNU) that governed South Africa between April 1994 and June 1996. Today, we look back on this period as one of the most productive and progressive in South African history, culminating in the adoption of a historic new Constitution in 1996. But the success of the GNU coalition, which included ministers from the ANC, NP and IFP, was never a sure thing. Just after the 1994 election, the *New York Times* described the GNU cabinet as 'an eclectic, even explosive, mix of personalities, backgrounds and styles that will challenge Mr Mandela's promise to govern by consensus'.[1] How did former enemies from the ANC, NP and IFP manage to turn the GNU into a success?[2]

Appointing the GNU cabinet

According to a formula contained in the 1993 interim Constitution, the April 1994 election results meant that the country's first democratic government would be a three-party coalition, with the president drawn from the ANC, while both the ANC and the

NP were entitled to appoint an executive deputy president. Based on their share of seats in the National Assembly, the ANC would have 18 ministers, the NP six, and the IFP three. Soon after the elections, the ANC named Thabo Mbeki as its deputy president, while the NP selected former president FW de Klerk.

Next, the coalition had to distribute the 27 cabinet portfolios among the three parties, and do so quickly. Even though the interim Constitution provided a detailed formula for assembling the cabinet, parties had to be matched with ministries, and people appointed to fill those positions. The interim Constitution empowered Mandela to appoint ministers 'after consultation with the executive deputy presidents and the leaders of the participating parties'.[3]

The president could also establish deputy ministerial posts, which would be allocated 'in the same proportion and according to the same formula' used for ministerial positions.[4] Years later, in his autobiography, De Klerk noted that the president had the final say about the portfolios each party received, but that party leaders had the authority to choose the ministers or deputy ministers for the portfolios allocated to their parties.[5] In an interview with the author in October 2016, De Klerk recalled that, although the negotiations over portfolios benefited from effective communication channels the leaders of the three parties had established during years of negotiations, 'the negotiations over which party would get which portfolios were tough'.[6]

The security portfolios were early sources of disagreement. Although the NP wanted to have one minister in each of what it regarded as the four main areas of government – security, economic, social, and administrative[7] – Mandela appointed ANC ministers to both of the security portfolios: defence, and safety and security. In the interview, De Klerk said his concerns had been assuaged by a compromise that made him chairman of the cabinet committee on security and intelligence affairs, 'which would give me an inside role with regard to the security ministries'.[8]

In an interview with the author in October 2016, the ANC's Sydney Mufamadi, whom Mandela appointed to head the safety and security ministry, said the group tried to work toward consensus, but that 'where there wasn't an agreement, there was an understanding that it would be the president's call. It required a balance between seeking consensus and deference to the president.'[9]

The ANC also insisted on controlling the foreign affairs ministry, and proposed that the outgoing NP minister, Roelof 'Pik' Botha, move to the minerals and energy portfolio. In contrast to the security portfolios, the party leaders agreed that the finance minister – Derek Keys – should remain in place in order to ensure continuity and credibility as South Africa worked to improve its economy. Per capita GDP had declined at an average rate of 1.3 per cent from 1985 to 1994.[10] 'It was going to take some time for the captains of industry to get used to the fact that [ANC ministers] were rational and literate in terms of economics,' Mufamadi recalled. 'They thought we were communists. Those who needed reassurances were therefore happy that there was a National Party minister – perhaps even that there was a white minister.'[11]

A final sensitive issue was an appropriate portfolio for IFP leader Mangosuthu Buthelezi. The party had presented the most serious threat to the electoral process in the lead-up to the national vote, because Buthelezi had demanded a postponement of the election and the establishment of a federal system, including a Zulu state. After the election, the IFP insisted that Buthelezi get a portfolio commensurate with his stature as leader of one of the three parties in the GNU. The IFP's position was reinforced by lingering fears that KwaZulu would return to violence if Buthelezi was not accommodated. But Buthelezi ultimately accepted Mandela's offer to become minister of home affairs, responsible for overseeing the upcoming 1995 municipal elections, and redesigning South Africa's national identity system.

According to Mufamadi, the parties agreed to provide some balance in politically sensitive portfolios by selecting deputy ministers whose political affiliations differed from those of their ministers. As a result, the ANC had deputy ministers in the NP-controlled portfolios of agriculture, finance, constitutional development, and welfare; the NP had deputies in the ANC-controlled land affairs, education, and justice ministries; and the IFP had a deputy in the ANC-controlled safety and security portfolio.[12] (Deputy ministers were not members of the cabinet.) In the final cabinet, the ANC controlled not only the powerful security and foreign affairs portfolios but also most of the key ministries involved in social service delivery: education, health, public enterprises, public works, and housing.[13]

Besides retaining control of the finance ministry, the NP also retained the agriculture ministry, a move that reflected the party's traditional base of rural Afrikaners, but this was balanced by the ANC's control over the ministry for land affairs. The NP chose Roelf Meyer, a key constitutional negotiator, for the important post of minister of constitutional development and provincial affairs, and filled the economically significant minerals and energy portfolio. The NP also controlled the smaller welfare and environmental affairs ministries, rounding out the party's six portfolios. Under the deal that saw Buthelezi become minister of home affairs, the IFP also secured the less influential ministries of correctional services and arts, culture, science, and technology. The GNU cabinet was sworn in on 11 May 1994 – just two weeks after the elections.

Overcoming early complications

The next key step in setting up the GNU coalition came a week after Mandela's inauguration when he appointed Professor Jakes Gerwel, a highly respected scholar and university administrator, to become director-general of the Office of the President, and to serve as cabinet secretary. Gerwel's appointment was a masterstroke. When tensions in the Cabinet rose, and tempers flared, Gerwel played an important – though largely unofficial – role in smoothing ruffled feathers and setting the antagonists back on the road to resolution.

Even though Gerwel had many weighty official responsibilities, he was widely praised for his personal characteristics. In an interview with the author in October 2016, Goolam Aboobaker, who served as head of cabinet research under Gerwel, recalled: 'There couldn't have been a better match [than that] between President Mandela and Jakes Gerwel. Gerwel was a very committed and humble person, and showed no political ambitions of his own. He made it clear that he was there only to provide a service for Mr Mandela. As a result, he was trusted by ANC and NP as well as IFP ministers.'[14]

In an interview with the author in September 2016, Roelf Meyer described Gerwel, who died in 2012, as 'the crucial person' in resolving many disputes. He had often worked with Gerwel to resolve confrontations. Ministers from the NP and the IFP were also keenly aware that 'Gerwel had the full confidence of Mandela, so he could take messages to Mandela like nobody else could'. [15]

In his interview with the author, FW de Klerk described Gerwel as 'very competent', adding, 'there was a genuine friendship between us. I think he accepted my bona fides, and I accepted his bona fides.'[16]

In an interview with the author in October 2016, Ahmed Kathrada, who had spent 26 years in jail with Mandela, and advised him during his presidency, later said NP ministers trusted Gerwel in part because 'he was as much Afrikaans-speaking as he was English-speaking . . . This helped him get along with NP ministers. He even got Mandela to include a poem by the Afrikaner poet Ingrid Jonker in his first state-of-the-nation address.'[17] Meyer said Gerwel's ability to gain the confidence of all sides made him the GNU's principal 'peacemaker'. This uniquely empowered him to undertake back-channel communication between all the different parties involved in a dispute, which often defused tensions without the need to directly involve senior political leaders.[18]

Despite Gerwel's role, the coalition was shaken by a series of early complications. In early July 1994, less than two months after Mandela's inauguration, the resignation of the influential NP finance minister, Derek Keys, rattled the nascent GNU. Although Keys cited personal reasons for his decision to leave the post, his departure threatened to upset the government's delicate political balance. But because both ANC and NP leaders recognised the need for an expert to handle the finance portfolio, the problem turned out to be less of a jolt than some had feared. Unable to identify a suitable replacement among Parliamentarians, Mandela and De Klerk agreed to designate the finance ministry as a non-partisan position, and to appoint a politically unaffiliated businessman, Chris Liebenberg, as Keys' successor. Liebenberg assumed the post in mid-September 1994.

Disputes over seemingly less significant matters also illuminated the sensitivities that lay just below the surface. Shortly after the appointment of the GNU coalition cabinet, tensions grew over the question of housing for Mandela and for De Klerk, the former president who now was a deputy president. De Klerk expected that he and his wife would be allowed to remain in the Libertas residence in Pretoria, where they had lived during his presidency, and that Mandela would take up residence in the presidential mansion in Pretoria, which had previously housed the ceremonial state president (a position that had been abolished). However, according to De Klerk, Mandela subsequently told him 'he was under great pressure from the ANC to move into Libertas, as that was seen to be the home of the head of government'.[19]

The two men agreed to swap residences, with the De Klerks moving into the presidential mansion. '[But] no sooner had we become used to the idea, [when Mandela] informed me that he was now under pressure from his senior colleagues to use the [presidential mansion] for other purposes.' As a result, the De Klerks had to change their plans for a third time and move to another official residence in Pretoria, which was in need of 'substantial refurbishing'. Although De Klerk wrote that he was personally 'indifferent' about the housing episode, his family was upset.[20] The confusion added to the pressures of the opening months.

Co-ordinating policy decisions

On the policy side of the equation, the GNU coalition had to agree on a common framework that fostered co-operation between the three parties. Because the ANC, NP, and IFP had developed divergent campaign platforms in the run-up to the election, reconciling their conflicting interests presented a potential stumbling block. To bridge policy gaps, the NP proposed a formal coalition agreement that spelled out each party's rights and responsibilities in detail. But the ANC argued that a policy agenda already existed in two forms: the interim Constitution, and the party's Reconstruction and Development Programme (RDP), which had formed the basis of its election manifesto, both of which many South Africans recognised and supported.

The interim Constitution listed 25 fundamental rights in areas ranging from education to labour relations, and 34 constitutional principles to guide the process of creating a final Constitution. 'We already had a script from which we read: the agreements we'd reached in the interim Constitution,' Mufamadi recalled. 'We didn't need a straitjacket, because we were leading the country on the basis of a common constitution.' Rather than a separate coalition agreement, 'we needed to persuade each other on a per-issue basis . . . If I have a proposal, I must be able to show that that proposal sits happily alongside the principles that anchor our Constitution.'[21]

Just as important, the ANC regarded its resounding electoral victory as an endorsement of the RDP as the policy framework for the GNU. The programme covered five key areas: meeting basic needs, developing human resources, building the economy, democratising the state and society, and arranging implementation. In practice, the NP and IFP shared most of the priorities laid out in the RDP. In his interview with the author, De Klerk explained that the NP supported the document 'because we did not have deep-rooted policy differences over what was necessary on the social welfare side'. For example, he noted, 'The NP was not against the expansion of housing [programmes] and the improvement of education.'[22]

In an interview with the author in September 2016, Bernie Fanaroff, an astrophysicist and former trade union activist who became head of the RDP office in the Presidency, said that, given the ANC's dominant position within the GNU, and the RDP's 'almost iconic status within society,' the programme encountered little opposition. He recalled: 'Everyone, including both the NP and IFP, was in fact very supportive. Everyone was in favour of a school feeding programme and building clinics, roads, and schools in the townships.'[23] The detailed negotiated agreements contained in the interim Constitution and the general agreement on the aims of the RDP meant that the two documents became the coalition cabinet's de facto governance agenda.

The next order of business for cabinet officials and their political principals was to create a system for running meetings of the politically diverse cabinet. On his first day as president, Mandela announced he would delegate the management of cabinet meetings to his two deputies, Mbeki and De Klerk, who would rotate

chairmanship of cabinet meetings every two weeks. This arrangement not only gave the two most powerful parties in the cabinet
equally important roles, but also kept the president elevated
above the partisan wrangling that was likely to take place during
cabinet meetings. According to Meyer, 'Mr Mandela never ran or
chaired the cabinet. He was there more as a guiding figure.'[24]
Thabo Mbeki later told interviewers that Mandela 'would very
rarely come to cabinet meetings, because he thought that whereas the rest of us attended to the practical matters of governing
the country, he must continue with the message of national
reconciliation and national unity'.[25]

Mandela's decision to delegate chairmanship of the cabinet
to his two deputies was a master stroke, on a number of levels.
First, he retained final authority because the interim Constitution stipulated that any decision made during a cabinet meeting
chaired by an executive deputy president had to be submitted
to the president for ratification.[26] Second, from an administrative
viewpoint, the move encouraged co-operation, and assigned clear
executive responsibility to both Mbeki and De Klerk. Perhaps
most importantly, the decision enabled Mandela to avoid direct
confrontations with De Klerk, with whom, understandably, he
had a tense relationship. Mbeki and De Klerk, on the other hand,
worked well together, and shared a keen interest in the details of
policy-making. 'There was no animosity or competition, and they
got along fairly well as individuals,' Meyer recalled.[27]

During cabinet meetings, ministers adopted the NP's established procedures – such as recording meetings and circulating
minutes within 48 hours – and reactivated three standing cabinet committees. Mandela appointed Mbeki to chair the economic

affairs committee, De Klerk to chair the security affairs committee, and the two shared the chairmanship of the social affairs committee on a two-week rotating basis. Mandela also assigned ministers to attend meetings of one of the three committees according to their portfolios. Recognising the need for communication and collegiality, the cabinet agreed that any minister could attend any committee meeting, and that all ministers would receive memorandums from all committee meetings.

The cabinet also set up standard procedures for the order of business at cabinet meetings. Mbeki later recalled: 'We inherited functioning state machinery, starting with the cabinet. When we sat in the cabinet, we conducted cabinet meetings according to how they did [it] during the apartheid years.'[28] The president was allowed to bring along anything from his desk to cabinet meetings, and both the executive deputy presidents had the same right. In an informal reflection of seniority within the coalition, Mbeki's turn to speak in cabinet came before De Klerk's, a practice that resulted in Mbeki becoming known as first executive deputy president, and De Klerk as the second.

Resolving disputes

Despite the creation of mechanisms for co-ordination within the coalition, policy disputes among the parties sometimes led to disagreements within the cabinet. In such cases, it was first up to the two chairmen to resolve the conflict. 'Both Mbeki and I smoked, so when things got too hot in the cabinet, we would often call for a smoke break,' De Klerk recounted. During the break, 'the ministers who were directly involved in the disagreement would then get together in light of the debate that had taken place, and oftentimes that would lead to a compromise'.[29]

If the chairmen were unable to engineer a compromise on a particularly thorny issue, cabinet officials and their political leaders often tried to resolve the dispute by setting up a multiparty, issue-specific negotiating committee. According to Aboobaker, such ad hoc cabinet committees represented the GNU's preferred approach: 'Cabinet would say, "this is a complicated issue, so let's form a ministers committee to try to address it".' If the ad hoc committee failed to generate agreement, the cabinet had the option to refer the dispute to another government branch.[30] In a chapter in a later book about post-conflict restructuring and development, Leon Wessels, deputy head of the constituent assembly, noted that Gerwel had identified three such issues on which the 'participating parties held fundamentally different positions of principle': abolishing the death penalty, legalising abortion, and establishing a truth and reconciliation commission (TRC) to investigate apartheid-era crimes.[31]

In an interview with the author in October 2016, Nicholas "Fink" Haysom, Mandela's primary legal adviser, said the coalition decided to 'presume the death penalty largely as a legal question as to whether it passed the standards set out in the new Constitution's bill of rights. For this position, there was some criticism of the jurisdiction of politics and, equally, the politicisation of the judiciary.'[32] In the face of political deadlock, with the NP and the IFP opposing and the ANC supporting the abolition of capital punishment, the government referred the decision to the country's newly established Constitutional Court, which ruled in mid-1995 that the death penalty was unconstitutional.

The question of legalising abortion, which was supported by the ANC and IFP but opposed by the NP, was similarly referred to another decision-making venue. In a cabinet memorandum in early 1995, the coalition approved the appointment of a Parliamentary committee to 'enquire into and report possible changes' to apartheid-era abortion legislation. At the same time, 'the parties represented in the GNU would reserve the right to argue their different positions on the matter' in Parliament.[33] Haysom said the abortion issue ignited 'a complex debate that also cut across purely political boundaries. Although the ANC supported it, members of Parliament were given the freedom to vote according to their consciences.'[34] Parliament settled the issue by legalising abortion in 1996.

The ANC's intention to create a TRC to investigate apartheid-era crimes created another flashpoint: 'We had tough negotiations with the ANC,' De Klerk wrote. 'They wanted more leniency for their fighters, and a stricter amnesty test for the [previously NP-aligned] security forces. We also pushed for greater focus on reconciliation.'[35] In keeping with the GNU coalition's established approach to dispute resolution, the cabinet created a committee, led by the justice minister and including ministers from all three parties, to 'conduct consultations and deliberations on this matter', according to a cabinet memorandum written by Gerwel in early 1995.[36]

Although the negotiations made significant progress, the talks failed to resolve disagreements about the powers and composition of the proposed commission. As a result, when the draft Promotion of National Unity and Reconciliation Bill was published for public comment, the ministerial committee also agreed to publish a joint media statement that reflected 'in a constructive manner the fact that the National Party and the Inkatha Freedom

Party hold reservations about the bill'.[37] Although the ANC made some concessions, its dominance in Parliament enabled the passage of the bill.

In an assessment of the stability of the GNU in late 1994, Gerwel told an interviewer: 'One would not be aware that it is a multi-party government if you were sitting in on the debates . . . You would not realise that people come from different parties.' He praised the level of civility and general agreement: 'It is an amazing thing to see people from different parties taking the same position on an issue.'[38] In his autobiography, published in 1999, De Klerk agreed: 'For the first year or so, the new cabinet functioned surprisingly smoothly.'[39]

The limits of consensus

But by early 1995, the 'consensus-seeking spirit' of the coalition government began to fracture. Disagreements over the final Constitution, which was scheduled for completion in May 1996, as well as tensions about the NP's role in the GNU and the need for the party to position itself before the 1999 national elections, contributed to a marked deterioration in the relationship between the two most powerful parties. On 18 January 1995, their leaders clashed openly for the first time during a cabinet meeting. ANC ministers were angry that, in the days leading up to the meeting, De Klerk had made a series of public statements that were critical of the ANC. At the same time, the NP contingent was concerned about 'the [party's] problem of simultaneously being part of the government but nevertheless also being the official opposition'.[40] The meeting escalated into a verbal altercation between Mandela and De Klerk, and the media got wind that De Klerk was 'seriously thinking of withdrawing from the GNU'.[41]

Two days after the acrimonious cabinet meeting, the two leaders met in Mandela's office in the Union Buildings, and De Klerk insisted on the need for a formal agreement that recognised the NP's right to criticise the government. De Klerk later wrote that Mandela was 'conciliatory, and he assured me that he wanted us to continue to work together in the GNU'.[42] During an impromptu media conference on the lawn of Mandela's residence, the two leaders announced they had 'cleared up the misunderstandings'.[43] But tensions about the NP's role in the coalition persisted. According to De Klerk, 'after about 15 or 18 months, the ANC felt they had now learned enough [about governance]. They also no longer accepted that the NP had a right to criticise decisions of cabinet that we disagreed with.'[44] By contrast, Mufamadi said that 'because the GNU cabinet was based on the principle of co-responsibility, we all had to defend its decisions'.[45]

In September 1995, the strains inherent in the power-sharing arrangement – with the ANC in a dominant position, and the NP a minority in government as well as the official opposition – finally boiled over. As recalled by De Klerk, he and Mandela were photographed at a public function in Johannesburg 'shaking our fingers at one another in a heated argument'.[46] De Klerk described the incident as both personal and political, calling Mandela's speech at the event a 'vicious attack on the National Party, which he worded in such a manner that it was clear that he had targeted me personally as the leader of the party . . . By this time, it was clear that the GNU was not working.'[47]

Internal NP politics heated up in the same period, adding fuel to the fire. 'Some people in the NP caucus – primarily those who were not in the cabinet – were more confrontational, and didn't like the continual compromises,' Meyer recalled.[48]

According to Mbeki, the NP was also increasingly coming under pressure from the DP – the DA's predecessor – which represented mainly whites, and held seven seats in the National Assembly. Due to the NP's involvement in the GNU, the DP 'said the National Party was betraying [white people] and selling them out . . . The National Party feared that the Democratic Party was taking away their constituency and electoral support,' Mbeki told his interviewers.[49]

Besides the deterioration in the personal relationship between Mandela and De Klerk, tensions between their two parties mounted further during negotiations over the wording of the final Constitution. Some NP ministers were unhappy about the ANC's refusal to accept permanent power-sharing. 'For the future, we wanted a consultative council of minority parties next to the cabinet. Such a council would operate as a consensus-seeking forum on issues of national importance,' De Klerk wrote.[50] But the ANC rejected the idea on the grounds that it would dilute democracy.

On 8 May 1996, the text of the final Constitution was adopted by 86 per cent of the members of the Constituent Assembly. Despite their reservations about the lack of a power-sharing provision, NP members voted in favour of the Constitution. While this was an historic moment, De Klerk announced just a week later that the NP would withdraw from the GNU coalition at the end of June 1996. In a speech, De Klerk said the reasons were that 'the Constitution contains no provision for the continuation of any form of joint decision making in the executive branch', and a perception among NP ministers 'that our influence within the GNU has been declining'.[51] But he also stressed that 'our decision should be seen as an important step in the growing maturity and normalisation of our young democracy'.[52] He added that internal NP dynamics had contributed to the decision: 'We had to position ourselves as an effective opposition party ahead of the 1999 election, and we couldn't do that if we were seen to be part of ANC decisions with which we did not agree.'[53]

The ANC acknowledged the legitimacy of the NP's decision. In a statement issued at the time, it said the decision 'reflects the fact that the National Party recognizes that our young democracy has come of age, and would need vigorous opposition unfettered by its participation in the executive. We respect their judgment on this matter as well as the party political considerations which precipitated their decision.'[54]

Haysom recalled that the decision did not come as a complete surprise. 'The implicit question was always: at what point before the next election will the NP withdraw? Even though some people thought it was too early [to withdraw in 1996], De Klerk exercised a political judgement. In other words, the question was how long a period would be necessary to share in the tasks of managing the transition, and what period would be necessary to create a new identity as an opposition party.'[55]

In the wake of the NP's withdrawal, IFP leader Mangosuthu Buthelezi also voiced his unhappiness with the GNU over political issues. In June 1996, he cited the ANC's failure to honour its 1994 pledge to hold international mediation as the 'major unresolved issue' between the two parties. Buthelezi also accused Mandela of treating the IFP with 'utter disdain . . . utter contempt', and described their relationship as 'tense'.[56] But despite widespread speculation that the IFP would withdraw from the GNU before the 1999 election, the minor alliance endured, with Buthelezi remaining in his position as home affairs minister until 2004.

In July 1996, ANC ministers replaced the six NP ministers who had withdrawn from the coalition cabinet, and the position of second executive deputy president, held by De Klerk, was abolished. The move did not disrupt the functioning of the cabinet. Although the Constitution allowed for the GNU to remain in force until the 1999 election, the NP's voluntary withdrawal marked the end of the coalition arrangement, both formally and in practice.

Despite its rather inglorious end, the GNU coalition had been remarkably stable during the two years of its existence. It had also managed to implement a raft of largely progressive reforms, including the adoption of a final Constitution, reforming the country's legal system and bureaucracy, creating nine new provinces, and integrating previously warring militias into a single national military.

Chapter Nine

The Cape Town coalition

Although much can clearly be learnt from the GNU experience, critics might point to the extraordinary political atmosphere that prevailed in South Africa at the time as a factor that made the GNU's success the exception rather than the rule. Given the historic nature of the transition away from apartheid, as well as the unprecedented international interest in the country, political leaders like Mandela, Mbeki, De Klerk and Buthelezi were under huge pressure to work together productively. Without entirely discarding these lessons, critics could ask whether there are any other examples where governing coalitions have functioned relatively smoothly and managed to improve governance *without* the added pressure of implementing a historical peace agreement under the watchful eye of the international community.

It is indeed a pertinent question. As the GNU coalition faded from the memories of most South Africans during the ensuing two decades of ANC hegemony, large parts of the country have become increasingly cynical about coalition governance. Safe in the knowledge that political intrigue and conflict always make for good headlines, media commentators and other analysts have honed in on the inherent instability of coalitions to construct a narrative that political alliances are doomed to failure. It is correct to say that South Africa's political graveyard contains numerous unsuccessful coalitions, but the story of sub-national coalitions since 1994 is not exclusively about failure.

It is not hard to find poor performers. Given the historical animosity between the two parties, the ANC-IFP coalition that governed KwaZulu-Natal during the late 1990s and early 2000s was fraught with tensions, and did little to stop that province's slide into maladministration. In the mid-2000s, the DA and IFP provincial 'coalition for change' also achieved very little, as infighting paralysed places like the Amajuba local municipality in KwaZulu-Natal. In 2000, the DP, NNP and the small Federal Alliance established a coalition in the Western Cape. But the arrangement ended in disaster only a year later, when the three parties attempted to merge. The deal collapsed, and between 2001 and 2004, the NNP governed in coalition with the ANC in the Western Cape before the NNP was eventually disbanded and absorbed into the ANC. Under both Western Cape coalitions, audit outcomes were poor, and levels of corruption high.

More recently, in June 2017, the DA-led minority council in Mogale City (Krugersdorp) collapsed when EFF and/or DA councillors betrayed their own parties' commitments to keep the ANC out of power. Using a secret ballot, an unknown group of councillors from the DA and/or EFF voted with the ANC to remove the DA from power, fuelling speculation about backroom deals and bribery. In the first ten months following the 2016 local elections, Mogale City had three different mayors from two different parties,[1] highlighting the instability that comes from the poor enforcement of co-operation agrccmcnts under a minority government.

Following the 2016 elections, the DA, UDM, COPE and ACDP created another formal coalition to govern Nelson Mandela Bay. After a year of halting progress, tensions flared in August 2017 when the municipal council voted to remove UDM member Mongameli Bobani as deputy mayor.[2] This came after the relationship between Bobani and DA mayor Athol Trollip had turned sour amid accusations that Bobani was involved in corruption, and had voted against the coalition during council meetings. Bobani's removal triggered a temporary crisis, but the coalition survived.

Given this list of examples, it is understandable that many media commentators and other analysts are sceptical of coalitions. But criticism becomes overly alarmist when commentators incorrectly extrapolate that coalitions are 'nigh impossible,' as one put it in mid-2017.[3] The multiparty coalition that governed Cape Town between 2006 and 2011 stands out as the most successful case of coalition governance in the country since the end of the GNU in 1996. It is a powerful example of how – even without the extraordinary circumstances that surrounded the GNU – coalitions can be made to work.

On a knife's edge

By March 2006, South Africa was already a very different country from the one governed by the GNU more than a decade earlier. The triumphant spirit of reconciliation that accompanied the GNU coalition had long since faded, replaced by stultifying one-party dominance. Nationally, the ANC was at the height of its powers, having secured a staggering 69.7 per cent of the vote in the 2004 election. Due to the NNP's decision to desert the DA through floor-crossing, the ANC even controlled the City of Cape Town, in the heartland of opposition politics.

But the ANC was in for a shock. On 3 March 2006, the IEC announced the following breakdown of results in Cape Town's 210-seat metropolitan municipal council election:[4]

DA: 609 545 votes; 41.85 per cent; 90 seats

ANC: 552 105 votes; 37.91 per cent; 81 seats

ID: 156 550 votes; 10.75 per cent; 23 seats

ACDP: 46 902 votes; 3.22 per cent; 7 seats

African Muslim Party (AMP): 19 316 votes; 1.33 per cent; 3 seats

UDM: 11 950 votes; 0.82 per cent; 2 seats

FF+: 7 170 votes; 0.49 per cent; 1 seat

Pan Africanist Congress (PAC): 7 108 votes; 0.49 per cent; 1 seat

United Independent Front (UIF): 3 472 votes; 0.24 per cent; 1 seat

Universal Party (UP): 2 346 votes; 0.16 per cent; 1 seat

With no party able to muster an outright majority of 106 seats, Cape Town was about to be governed by a coalition. But by which combination of parties? With a DA-ANC coalition politically out of the question, there were essentially four possibilities. A coalition between the DA and ID would be fairly straightforward, yielding a majority of 113 seats (90 + 23 = 113/106). But the ID could also opt to work with the ANC, in which case the two parties would only have 104 seats (81 + 23 = 104/106) – two shy of a majority. The second option was thus a coalition of at least three parties built around the ANC-ID axis.

The third possibility was a DA-led coalition that included all parties except the ANC and ID, which would yield a majority of 106 (90 + 7 + 3 + 2 + 1 + 1 + 1 + 1 = 106/106). (Importantly, even if the ANC similarly formed a coalition with all parties except the DA and ID, it would only control 97 seats $(81 + 7 + 3 + 2 + 1 + 1 + 1 + 1 = 97/106$ – still nine short of a majority.) The fourth possibility was that no parties agreed to form a coalition, and would opt for a minority government instead.

Option 1: DA-ID coalition $(90 + 23 = 113/106)$

Option 2: ANC-ID-other(s) coalition $(81 + 23 + X = 106/106)$

Option 3: DA-ACDP-AMP-UDM-FF+-PAC-UIF-UP coalition $(90 + 7 + 3 + 2 + 1 + 1 + 1 + 1 = 106/106)$

Option 4: No coalition (possible minority government)

Under section 45 of the Municipal Structures Act, the first council meeting had to take place within 14 days of the election,[5] which meant the parties had until 15 March 2006 to agree on a coalition. According to Gareth van Onselen, who later published an insightful essay about the coalition negotiations, many observers initially overlooked the possibility that option three – a DA-led coalition which excluded the ID – could come to pass: 'Instead, either of the opinion it was an impossibility or by simply failing to do the maths, [the media] continued to describe the ID as holding the balance of power.'[6]

Sealing the deal

Negotiations kicked off on 4 March 2006, with the DA and ANC holding a courtesy meeting. Ryan Coetzee, former CEO of the DA, and a member of its negotiating team, later recalled: 'We had this hilarious meeting with the ANC, where we set out our position. We wanted the mayoralty and control of the executive committee, which clearly they were never going to agree to. And they said, very politely, "Oh, that is very nice, our position is we want the mayoralty and control of the executive committee." And we said, very politely, "Oh, okay, thank you. Well, we can't agree to that." And then everybody said, "Well, it looks like we can't agree but, you know, thanks for the chat." And off we all went.'[7]

Next, the DA turned to the ID. The DA team – mainly comprising Coetzee and James Selfe – tried to persuade the ID that its voters would desert it if the party partnered with the ANC, which had just been rejected by the electorate. But the ID would have none of this. In exchange for its co-operation, it wanted the DA to commit itself to replacing Cape Town's executive mayoral system with an executive committee system, which would dilute the powers of the mayor, as it would probably have created a mayoral committee comprising councillors from the DA, ANC and ID. This would have made it extremely difficult for the council to take decisions, effectively deadlocking the municipality, and giving the ID a permanent veto. According to Patricia de Lille, who led the ID at the time, 'We had approaches by the ANC, we had approaches by the DA, but we still insisted, very naively at the time, that we wanted to have this executive committee system.'[8]

Despite the fact that the DA had also spoken about the need for a committee system during the election campaign, the party now rejected the ID's notion. The reason was simple: under a committee system, the mayoral committee would have featured four DA councillors, four ANC councillors, and two ID councillors – essentially creating a hung government. The DA made it clear that it would not budge. In contrast, while the creation of a committee system (which would give it a veto over important decisions) appeared to be the ID's formal line in the sand, the party's negotiations in practice were guided more by a desire to gain access to state resources.

Another difference between the DA and ID strategics was that whereas the DA did not directly involve the party's caucus in the city or even its mayoral candidate, Helen Zille, in the negotiations, the ID's negotiating team – consisting of Simon Grindrod, Avril Harding and David Sassman – continually consulted all the ID's councillors. 'We had 23 councillors, and as all these things were going on, I consulted all the time with the 23 councillors, and, for me, with hindsight, therein lay the problem,' De Lille told Van Onselen.[9]

The ANC made the ID an offer, which De Lille presented to her caucus. In the ANC's rush to hang on to power at all costs, it made the ID a lucrative offer. It not only offered the ID a number of positions on the Cape Town council, including the deputy mayoralty, but also a range of other powerful positions in municipalities across the Western Cape. In exchange, the ID had to give up its demand for a veto in the form of a committee system. While the ID had insisted on a committee system in its negotiations with the DA, this quickly melted away in the face of the ANC's tempting offer. De Lille regretted that the 23 ID councillors were 'part of the negotiations. And so the DA offered a package, and the ANC offered a package. And then there was to-ing and fro-ing between the two packages, with the interested group, the 23 councillors. And you know how people are. The ANC package looked better . . . *Hulle oë word almal groot* [their eyes got bigger and bigger].'[10]

With media coverage largely focused on the ID, the DA quietly changed tack. One week before the deadline, the DA team met all of the smaller opposition parties (thus excluding the ANC and ID). Coetzee described the meeting to Van Onselen: 'The ACDP had done a bit of work to round up quite a lot of the smaller parties, but at that point we thought it was too fragile. We thought it would be a nightmare government that would fall apart. You know, how do you keep seven parties together when they are so fundamentally different? So we didn't take it too seriously, but we had a nice meeting with them.'[11]

However, with the ID apparently determined to join the ANC, and with only four days to go before the legally mandated vote in council, the DA realised that a multiparty coalition (option three) was its only pathway to power. Building on the foundation laid by Pauline Cupido from the ACDP,[12] the DA got together with the minor parties to try to iron out a coalition agreement. The negotiations were led by Selfe, who wrote up the agreement in a four-page document. The first issue was to create a framework for sharing posts among the partners. In an interview with the author in July 2017, Zille recalled: 'Our bottom line was that the DA had to have the finance and corporate services portfolios, because we have to make sure that people are appointed on the right basis, and that the finances are run honestly. We wanted those two transversal departments. But everything else had to be negotiable.'[13]

Zille also recalled that it was difficult to give up two other vital departments: economic development, and community safety. 'The AMP [Africa Muslim Party] insisted on having the department of economic development, while the UDM insisted on having community safety. It was a huge deal to give those up, but we did.'[14] After a series of tough negotiations, the prospective partners agreed to a form a Mayco (shorthand for mayoral committee). Besides the mayoralty, the DA would get five portfolios, including finance and corporate services. The ACDP would get the position of deputy mayor, while the FF+ would get the speaker, and each of the other four parties would get one Mayco position each. The city's 20 well-paid sub-council positions, as well as its 15 bargaining council and Local Government Association executive seats, would also be equally distributed among the partners, with the DA's Coetzee noting that 'literally every councillor from those other parties got something'.[15]

The coalition agreement also referred specifically to the principles and values that would guide the metro government's work. The negotiators agreed to establish a leadership committee to 'enhance co-operation and mutual trust', and to resolve disputes. Cognisant of the fact that the coalition included liberals and conservatives as well as Christian and Muslim fundamentalists, the document noted that 'this committee will meet at the request of any leader to discuss any aspect relating to the administration of the council'.[16] In the case of 'a serious moral or principled objection to any matter or where it was impossible to reach consensus, the party retained the right to disagree with or criticize the majority viewpoint, within council and outside it'.[17]

However, only the DA, ACDP, UDM, FF+, UIF, and UP immediately signed the agreement. The PAC and AMP were now the key spoilers of the DA's plan. With less than 72 hours to go before the mayoral election, the DA accepted that the PAC would not enter the coalition. The best it could hope for was to convince the party's lone councillor to abstain from voting. While the AMP seemed open to joining the coalition, it delayed signing on the dotted line. With only one day left before the decisive vote, the DA's Kent Morkel finally managed to convince the AMP's three councillors to join the alliance. Van Onselen described this breakthrough as follows:

> The AMP's agreement was critical. And the DA was right to be worried. The ANC, like the DA, had realised the AMP's three votes could be all-important and had, in the interim, approached the party to do a deal. It had calculated that, together with the ID, it had 107 votes and everything it needed to secure the mayoralty. The AMP had responded favourably. But the ANC had not taken into account the AMP's hostility towards the ANC among its members. Much of this could be traced back to [former ANC mayor Nomaindia] Mfeketo, whose controversial adviser, Blackman Ngoro, had done a great deal to alienate coloured voters over the past year. And it was Morkel who had led the charge against him publicly on the DA's behalf. He was perfectly positioned to convince. After Morkel's intervention, the AMP put the DA's offer to its councillors and was soon endorsed as the most politically sensible option for the party. It had played the ANC, but the ANC would not realise this until the next day . . . Late in the day, all seven parties reached a final agreement.[18]

The first order of business on 15 March 2006, the day of the vote, was to elect a new council speaker. From the seven-party coalition side, the UP nominated Dirk Smit of the FF+, who went up against the ANC's Gavin Paulse. Smit won by a single vote, indicating that the coalition was holding together, and that the writing was on the wall. The ANC was shaken to the core, and called for two adjournments. The ANC caucus cornered the lone councillor from the PAC, Bennett Joko, as well as the AMP's three councillors in a last-ditch effort to convince them to vote in favour of the ANC's mayoral and deputy mayoral candidates.

After a 50-minute delay, the council finally reconvened to elect the mayor, with the DA's Helen Zille squaring off against the ANC incumbent, Nomaindia Mfeketo. Zille won by 106 to 103 votes. This showed that both the AMP and the PAC had held firm despite the pressure applied – and enticements offered – by the ANC. With the PAC's Joko abstaining, the coalition's final score of 106 votes meant that someone from the ANC or ID had also broken ranks and voted for the DA. In the final vote of the day, the coalition's Andrew Arnolds (ACDP) defeated the ID's Simon Grindrod by a single vote to become deputy mayor. After two weeks of arduous negotiations, the seven-party coalition took control of Cape Town, with the ANC and ID on the opposition benches.

Governing together

With the negotiating teams having played their part, it now fell to mayor Helen Zille to keep the coalition together and translate political co-operation into better metro governance. With a mayoral committee in place, the metro government's first priority was to halt the corruption that had taken root under the ANC. According to Zille, the scale of the challenge was overwhelming:

> The city's middle management had been hollowed out, ANC cadres had been deployed to many top positions, and the finances were precarious. Above all, the tender

system was susceptible to serious abuse and mani-
pulation. I was amazed to learn that the ANC had restruc-
tured the administration to make the same 'cadre'
responsible for both procurement and legal compliance . . . Unsurprisingly, the person who headed both
offices was widely known as Mr Ten Per Cent. It was
alleged that this was the cut he required to swing a
tender in the desired direction . . . After a rudimentary
investigation, it was clear that his services would . . .
have to be terminated.[19]

But the decision to clean up the tender process and get rid of
Mr Ten Per Cent threatened the coalition. It turned out that his
brother was a UDM councillor in the neighbouring municipality
of Stellenbosch, where the UDM was also in coalition with the
DA. 'If we terminated Mr Ten Per Cent's contract, we were warned,
his brother would bring down the government [of Stellenbosch],
and the UDM might be forced to withdraw from Cape Town's
multiparty government as well,' Zille wrote. If the UDM left, the
coalition would fall. But after a disciplinary process, the council
followed through and dismissed Mr Ten Per Cent in January
2007. 'By that time we had done a lot of preparatory work and
the UDM, both in Stellenbosch and Cape Town, held firm in their
respective coalitions.'[20]

In its effort to clean up the tendering system, the council also
decided to scrap one of the key rules that facilitated corruption.
The previous ANC administration had adopted a rule which prohibited any company that was not at least 30 per cent black-
owned from even tendering for a government contract. In practice,

the rule suppressed competition, and allowed the ANC council to channel contracts to its network of cronies. Although the DA in the city expected a massive outcry to follow the decision to do away with the 30 per cent quota rule, Zille recalled that there 'wasn't even a peep about it'.[21] She ascribed the surprising lack of resistance to the fact that all the DA's coalition partners knew that the rule was only benefiting a handful of ANC cronies, 'so everyone was happy when I said, let's introduce a system to eradicate that. That actually smoothed the way.'[22] The proposal to scrap the rule was passed.

Next, the council introduced greater transparency as another means of counteracting corruption. The municipality opened bid adjudication committees and Mayco meetings to the public, which enabled Capetonians to watch their elected officials deliberate and make decisions. After a lengthy struggle to remove the ANC-aligned city manager, Wallace Mgoqi – who fraudulently tried to collapse the coalition shortly after it was elected[23] – Zille appointed Achmat Ebrahim, an experienced technocrat who was respected by councillors from across the political spectrum.[24]

Led by DA councillor Belinda Walker, the corporate services department drew up a new set of human resources rules, job descriptions, reporting lines, and payment and benefit scales, which created a merit-based appointment system and enabled the city to begin to hold employees accountable for their performance.[25] The city introduced two further early innovations: the C3 tracking system for handling citizen complaints, and a performance management dashboard. While the complaints system improved the city's ability to respond to problems, the dashboard enabled it to adhere to its planning priorities by continually monitoring the activities of all city departments.[26]

Although the coalition partners were generally supportive of the moves to depoliticise and reform the city's bureaucracy, councillors were much less willing to cede control over appointments in their own offices. Some strenuously objected to a suggestion that staff in their own offices should also be subject to the merit-based appointment process implemented in the city. Zille decided not to push back too hard. 'At the time, each Mayco member had about three or four positions in their own offices which they could fill at their own discretion,' she recalled. 'The way I balanced it out was to say that as long as you go through the right processes, you can appoint your own little network [in your private office], but outside of that, the stringent HR rules applied.'[27]

The effect was to confine possible patronage to councillors' private (political) offices, while ensuring that non-political officials were appointed on the basis of competence. Councillors thus had a relatively free hand to appoint their own office managers, media liaison officers and secretaries – but these people could only remain in their positions while the councillor was in office. For Zille, the key question was 'whether it is make or break if someone chooses an unqualified person to be their private secretary or media liaison? The answer was no, because [the effect] was not going to extend further than their own office. If you appoint useless people, your office won't run, so only you will suffer the consequences.'[28] The decision was emblematic of the need to balance civil service reform with the political imperatives of a coalition government.

Zille soon realised that 'sometimes you have to pay for symbols to hold onto substance . . . On the stipulation that it must all go through the proper process, if people want a fridge in their office, give them a fridge. If people want to drive a council car, just give them a car. These things are not costless, but they do take away the possibility of the other side [the ANC] tempting coalition partners away with patronage offers.'[29] But it was equally important to know where to draw the line. In fact, while the coalition council made surprisingly quick progress on substantive reforms, it was a clash over a seemingly peripheral issue of style that posed the first real threat to the coalition.

In the process of deciding which Mayco members would get which offices in the Cape Town Civic Centre, the ACDP's deputy mayor wanted to install an en-suite toilet in his new office. However, because the building's plumbing system would have to be extended to connect the toilet, this would cost more than R1 million. Zille 'just laughed it off, and assumed everyone else would too'.[30] Fortunately, the coalition agreement had created a forum where the smaller parties (excluding the DA) could discuss problems informally before taking it to the coalition management committee. According to Zille, 'It helped enormously to have a separate forum with just the coalition partners so they can talk through their issues. For example, this toilet issue was one that came up at this separate forum. I didn't know about this toilet issue that was just about to bring down the government.'[31]

After a meeting between the smaller parties, the FF+'s Dirk Smit, who served as speaker in the coalition-led council, went to Zille's office. Smit told her: 'This is a serious issue, and you need to treat it as such . . . I am not exaggerating when I tell you that this could bring down the coalition.'[32] As a result, Zille softened her approach and held a series of meetings with her Mayco over the matter. Although the deputy mayor ultimately did not get his

R1 million toilet, the less dismissive posture adopted by Zille prevented the coalition from derailing over a seemingly trivial dispute. In her autobiography, Zille wrote: 'It was my first real lesson in the *realpolitik* of coalition management'.[33]

But the next clash was already on the horizon. Due to the DA's overwhelming majority compared to its partners, as well as the public visibility of the mayor, an (accurate) perception quickly developed among the smaller parties that the DA was dominating the coalition. Zille acknowledged that 'the DA got huge publicity, and the partners got almost none. They didn't like that, because they didn't want to be in a coalition to be drowned out by the DA, they wanted to be in a coalition to be in government and build their own bases for the future.' This soon became a sticking point during coalition meetings.

Zille's response was again to give 'a lot of leeway on things that didn't go down to substance or principle. I tried to give them more publicity, but that's where I clashed with my own party's federal head office.'[34] The DA's party leadership was uncomfortable with the notion of ceding publicity to its partners, but Zille insisted that 'it was essential for the partners to get publicity if they were to stay in [the coalition]'.[35] When the city launched new projects or held media events, Zille consequently went out of her way to invite Mayco members from the partner parties, even declining some invitations so that the DA did not steal all of the limelight.[36]

Adapting to change

By early 2007, the coalition government had made significant progress on some important issues. However, the fact that the coalition had a majority of only one seat in the council left it very vulnerable. In her interview, Zille admitted that 'it was a very bad psychological state to start in, because we didn't think [the coalition] would last . . . When people don't think they're going to be secure in their positions, they are very anxious and look around for any bolthole that can make them more secure.'[37]

While it had managed to overcome a series of earlier challenges, the seven-party coalition ran into serious trouble about nine months into its term. The root of the problem was that one of the coalition councillors, Badih Chabaan from the AMP, was secretly working with the ANC on a plan to defect, and thereby overthrow the metro government. Chabaan's opposition to the coalition was purely opportunistic. Right from the start, he had insisted on controlling the economic development department with an eye toward securing contracts for the 2010 FIFA World Cup. When the coalition blocked these attempts, Chabaan resolved to put an ANC-led coalition in power. In return, the ANC offered him the position of deputy mayor, along with the responsibility for overseeing all preparations for the World Cup. The switch would have paved the way for Chabaan's nefarious intentions.

The DA realised that the AMP was on its way out, and that the coalition would collapse. But it had a new card up its sleeve. According to Zille, by early 2007, ID leader 'Patricia de Lille had realised what a political *faux pas* she had made [by siding with the ANC and rejecting a coalition with the DA], so she had a massive interest in getting out of the alignment with the ANC'.[38] Zille began negotiating with De Lille about the ID replacing the AMP in the coalition, thereby giving the metro government a solid majority.

Even though the DA and ID could easily have governed on their own (they would have controlled 113 of the council's 210 seats), Zille had a longer-term goal in mind. 'I told Patricia that we could not ditch the smaller parties, because I knew our credibility was critical down the line if we wanted to make future coalitions. We had to make our coalition partners believe that we were not just fair weather friends. If we don't establish a trend of being principled partners, in the future when coalitions come to places like Nelson Mandela Bay, who is going to come to us?'[39]

Although the DA and ID would both have secured many more Mayco positions if they dumped the smaller parties, they had the foresight to keep the multiparty coalition going. The plan worked. On 16 January 2007, the coalition expelled Chabaan's AMP[40] and brought the ID on board, securing 126 of 201 council seats. With a solid coalition agreement and a secure majority in place, the risk of the coalition collapsing dissipated, making it much easier for the council to implement its shared agenda. The coalition comfortably saw out the rest of its term until May 2011, when the DA won an outright majority in Cape Town, and no longer needed to govern in coalition.

Under the 2006 to 2011 coalition government, Cape Town was transformed from a dysfunctional municipality into the top performer in the country. For example, the city increased capital investment in infrastructure from US$161 million to US$806 million, while annual expenditure on maintenance also doubled. The total value of the city's maintenance backlog was reduced to only 11 per cent of the annual maintenance budget – the lowest ratio of any metro in the country.[41]

A 2011 paper from Princeton University's Innovations for Successful Societies research programme reported that:

The stabilization of the city's bureaucracy greatly en-
hanced capacity. By 2009, the city was spending over
95 per cent of its budget . . . Whereas the bureaucratic
chaos of prior years had blocked staff training and
development and led the city to under-spend allocated
resources on this function, [the coalition] increased the
percentage of the city's staff-training budget spent to
94 per cent from 80 per cent . . . By 2010, most rankings
of South African metropolitan areas rated Cape Town as
having the country's best government. The city received
unqualified audits, signifying that it had spent its budget
well and fully disclosed its financial circumstances at a
time when many other local governments and agencies
did not. The central government's Auditor-General
praised the city's sound financial management in 2009,
and the city's credit rating improved. The management
team also won the support of private investors, as
indicated by its ability to float successful bond issues.[42]

By the end of its term, the Cape Town coalition stood out as an
exceptional home-grown example of not only how to manage
and keep a coalition government together, but also how to build
a capable bureaucracy and engineer good governance under a
multiparty administration.

Chapter Ten

Making coalitions work

Before extracting deeper insights from the GNU and Cape Town stories, it's important to acknowledge that the two cases differed in some respects. First, the two stories obviously played out in different spheres of government: while the GNU was about a national coalition that governed the entire country, the Cape Town coalition was in charge of a single metro. The two coalitions also operated in different political climates. While the GNU came to power amid the euphoria and tolerance that accompanied the transition to democracy, the Cape Town coalition emerged in a much more hostile political environment marked by increasing corruption and aggressive partisanship.

A close look at the incentives faced by the different coalitions reveals a further important distinction. Although the interim Constitution gave both the NP and IFP the legal right to participate in the GNU – and although the ANC wanted the NP and IFP to participate for the sake of stability – the ANC did not need the votes of two partner parties to implement its legislative agenda. Throughout the GNU's two-year lifetime, the ANC could always fall back on its 62 per cent majority in the National Assembly, which meant that when push came to shove, it could unilaterally enact its agenda even in the face of resistance from the NP and IFP.

In Cape Town, the DA never had this luxury. Throughout the coalition's five years in power, the DA remained dependent on support from its coalition partners to enact bylaws, rules, and other legislative changes. In the GNU, the ANC could ultimately afford to alienate its coalition partners and still remain in power – as happened in mid-1996, when the NP quit. By contrast, the DA would have immediately lost power in Cape Town if it was abandoned by its partners.

Despite these differences, the two coalition tales also display some striking commonalities. Before turning to the question of society's role in fostering strong coalitions, the first part of this chapter draws out the similarities between the GNU and Cape Town stories, and distils them into a number of concrete recommendations to coalition leaders. As South Africa's two most successful coalition governments to date, what lessons can we take from the GNU and Cape Town experiences?

Negotiation: the seed of success

The first challenge facing coalitions is to constitute a government. Depending on the sphere of governance (national, provincial or municipal), the first step in formally establishing a government is for a simple majority of representatives in a relevant legislature (national Parliament, provincial Parliament or municipal council) to elect a president, premier or mayor. Once an executive leader has been elected, the second step is for them to announce the composition of their executives.

Although the Constitution spells out the formal process for establishing executives in all three spheres of government, the formalities are preceded by a set of coalition negotiations. This process involves three steps: getting preliminary buy-in from prospective coalition partners; dividing jobs among the different partner parties; and translating an informal deal into a formal coalition agreement. This is where the real work of assembling a coalition government takes place.

The comparison between the GNU and Cape Town is instructive. In terms of the 1993 interim Constitution, the NP and IFP both had the right to join the GNU cabinet because both parties had garnered more than 10 per cent of the national vote. This meant that there was no need for the ANC to identify its coalition partners. But the GNU was an exception in this regard.

When it comes to the process of assembling a coalition government, the Cape Town story is more apposite. Like all of the coalitions we will see in the future, no single party had a legal right to form a government in Cape Town after the 2006 election had produced a hung council. Indeed, at the very heart of the coalition system is the assumption that only a party that garners an outright majority of 50 per cent plus one has a legal *right* to govern. If no single party achieves a majority of 50 per cent – as happened in Cape Town in 2006 – the government is up for grabs to any combination of parties able to cobble together a majority.

The Cape Town case illustrates one of the key shifts that coalitions will engineer in South African politics: when no party gets more than 50 per cent, size begins to matter less, and comparatively minor parties become far more powerful than under single-party rule. As we saw in the previous chapter, the DA and ANC respectively won 41.85 per cent and 37.91 per cent of the vote in Cape Town's 2006 election. However, from a legal point of view, the DA did not have any greater right than the ANC to form a metro government. If the ANC and ID managed to convince one more party to join its coalition, it would have had a 50 per cent majority. Had that happened, it would have been perfectly legal for the ANC-led coalition to take over the municipality even though the DA had won more votes during the election.

It is worth reflecting on another example of how being the biggest party in a legislature becomes less significant if that party does not reach the 50 per cent threshold. During the 2016 municipal elections, the ANC won the most votes in Johannesburg, with 44.99 per cent. The DA came second, with 38.40 per cent. When the results were announced, the headline of a News24 report stated that the 'ANC takes Joburg, but gets below 50%'[1] This is a glaring contradiction in terms, and a good example of how sensationalist or sloppy reporting can misshape voter expectations. The second part of the statement – that the ANC got below 50 per cent – completely negates the statement that it 'took' Johannesburg. Even though the ANC got the most votes in the Johannesburg metro, the fact that it fell short of a majority meant that it could not govern the city on its own.

Despite the DA only being the second-biggest party in the Johannesburg council, it ultimately assembled a DA-led minority government that took control of the city. Having fallen short of the 50 per cent mark, the ANC's majority counted for very little because it failed to broker a deal with other parties. In circumstances where no party garners an outright majority, expert negotiators become the most powerful tools in any political party's arsenal. The ANC did not lose Cape Town (or Johannesburg) because it won fewer votes than the DA. The ANC lost because the DA out-negotiated it.

In coalition governments around the world, it is often the behind-the-scenes work of negotiators that seals the deal. The Netherlands provides a fascinating example of the central role played by coalition negotiators. This coalition-based society, where no single party has governed alone since 1945, has developed an institution dedicated solely to forming coalitions. Following the outcome of a Dutch election (which inevitably ends in a hung legislature), the lower house of Parliament officially appoints a specific person – usually a widely respected representative of the party that got the most votes – to the position of *informateur,* or *verkenner* [scout].

This person is tasked with exploring the various coalition possibilities produced by the election result, and conveying these to political leaders. Once the *informateur* finds a combination of political leaders willing to establish a coalition government that can muster a majority in Parliament, he or she draws up a preliminary coalition agreement and informs the lower house, which then appoints another person – usually the leader of the biggest party, and therefore the likely incoming prime minister – to the position of *formateur.* Whereas the *informateur* is tasked with getting in principle buy-in for a coalition deal, it is up to the *formateur* to formalise the agreement through the sharing of cabinet portfolios.[2]

Though much less organised than the entrenched and stable Dutch system, the same basic process played itself out in Cape Town. The DA tasked trusted lieutenants such as Ryan Coetzee and James Selfe to explore all the possibilities and to engage with all different possible partners (including the ANC) with an eye toward forming a viable majority. In Cape Town, the break-through came when the ACDP's Pauline Cupido convened a meet-ing between the DA and the smaller parties. At that meeting, the DA got informal buy-in from its prospective partners.

But an informal deal is only the first step. Coalitions are often at their most vulnerable when the different parties try to move from an informal deal to a formal agreement. In the shift from an informal 'I think we can work together' to putting pen on paper, coalition leaders face the difficult challenge of sharing executive functions among the different partners. Like the seven-party coalition in Cape Town, the GNU also faced the challenge of shar-ing executive positions in a way that promoted service delivery, and built a cohesive cabinet.

While there is no firm recipe for deciding how to share execu-tive functions among different parties, the two case studies reveal that this is essentially a two-step process. The first requirement is to agree on *how many* portfolios each party would get, followed by agreeing on *who* should fill those portfolios. Here again we see that the GNU had an advantage over the Cape Town coalition, because the interim Constitution contained a detailed formula that used the election results to specify how many portfolios each party would get (ANC 18, NP six and IFP three). (The interim Con-stitution also limited the number of cabinet positions to 27 – a cap that doesn't exist in the current Constitution.)

While the Cape Town coalition had to create its own power-sharing formula, the task was simplified because the Municipal Structures Act specified that a maximum of 10 councillors could serve on the Mayco.[3] With Zille as mayor, the coalition agreed to create the maximum of 10 portfolios, giving five to the DA (including the powerful finance and corporate services positions), while the smaller parties shared the remaining five portfolios, and the FF+ got the position of council speaker. Because the ACDP was the second biggest party in the coalition, it also got the additional position of deputy mayor. In the process of sharing portfolios, the DA sacrificed the significant economic development portfolio, which went to the AMP, as well as the important community safety portfolio, which went to the UDM.

The GNU coalition reflected similar dynamics. While the ANC took control of the security apparatus, foreign affairs, and most major service delivery portfolios, the NP held on to the powerful finance and constitutional development ministries. In turn, the IFP would not be satisfied with anything less than the ministry of home affairs. What both these cases make clear is that political leaders usually attempt to divide portfolios in a way that reflects the power dynamics within the coalition. In turn, the power dynamics are shaped by election outcomes. Therefore, the challenge for negotiators and their principals is to translate the balance of power created by election results into a concrete distribution of power within the executive.

With agreement on which parties would control which portfolios, the next task is to fill those positions with specific people. In both the GNU and Cape Town cases, it was up to the various party leaders to decide on who would fill their respective portfolios. Although there can be exceptions – such as Mandela and De Klerk's joint decision to replace Derek Keys with Chris Liebenberg as finance minister – leaders of one partner party are usually not allowed to interfere in the selection of candidates by another party. The GNU case provides a final intriguing example of how to potentially generate fruitful co-operation within the different portfolios. In a number of important ministries, the GNU partners agreed that the deputy minister would come from a different party than the minister. This example was also enthusiastically adopted a decade later in Kenya's grand coalition, when every portfolio was 'balanced out' in this way.[4] If the minister came from party A, the cabinet secretary (Kenya's equivalent of a director-general) was appointed by party B.

Once the prospective partners informally agree to co-operate and devise a politically acceptable cabinet structure, the final step is usually to codify the agreement. In this regard, the GNU provides an important countervailing example, because the ANC refused to adopt a formal agreement to guide the coalition's work. The failure to codify the relationship among the different partners contributed to the eventual breakdown of the coalition, because there was no agreed set of rules and procedures for handling disagreements.

This is a vital point. Formal coalition agreements define how future disputes will be handled, and the circumstances under which a coalition partner may be disciplined or even expelled. The agreement usually also creates a number of formal mechanisms, such as coalition management committees, where grievances can be aired. As was the case with the Cape Town coalition, these documents should also state how criticism will be handled. Should partners be allowed to publicly criticise decisions they disagree with? Or should all criticism be handled internally, for the sake of presenting a united front? Lastly, coalition agreements should specify the broad basic values that guide the work of the government. For example, do all partners agree to abide by the parameters outlined in the Constitution? These are all questions that are best resolved in a formal agreement before a coalition assumes office.

Political parties can take a number of steps to prepare for the rigours of coalition negotiations, where having the in-house talent to handle complex multiparty discussion will be vital. The first is to invest in training a cohort of negotiators who are versed in the country's electoral laws. But coalition negotiators need more than legal knowledge; they also need to have the emotional intelligence required to understand the motivations of their prospective coalition partners. In a description of James Selfe's role during the formation of the Cape Town coalition, Ryan Coetzee explained how coalition lieutenants need to combine a keen legal mind with emotional intelligence: 'James Selfe is calm, tactically astute, unfailingly polite to his adversaries, and a master draftsman of political documents.'[5] This list of attributes could well serve as a job description for coalition negotiators, and political leaders should use it to identify their future master negotiators.

Another useful way for parties to prepare for the coalition era is through scenario planning. Parties could host workshops where political leaders are required to play out different coalition scenarios. Tasks like ranking the importance and appropriateness of different cabinet ministries would also serve to prepare parties for the trade-offs inherent to coalition negotiations. Having a ranked set of priority ministries as well as a clear understanding of the dynamics at play during negotiations can put a party at a distinct advantage over less prepared rivals. Parties that have the foresight to invest in specialist negotiators, training work-shops, and scenario planning will soon reap the rewards of more favourable and stable coalition deals.

Reading from the same script

The GNU largely relied on the RDP to guide its policies, while the partners also agreed that the interim Constitution should serve as the ultimate reference point for all policy choices. However, both the GNU and Cape Town coalitions would have benefited from a more detailed and explicit description of their shared poli-cy agendas. Kenya provides a useful example.

After Kenya's grand coalition assumed power in early 2008, one of the key challenges it faced was to agree on policy priorities. Lingering animosity between the Mwai Kibaki and Raila Odinga camps had created a risk of deadlock in cabinet decision-making in the absence of a strong unifying agenda. The two parties repre-sented in the coalition – Kibaki's Party of National Unity (PNU), and Odinga's Orange Democratic Movement (ODM) – had conducted their election campaigns on the basis of two distinct manifestos.

In an interview with the author in September 2015, Odinga re-called that, when he became prime minister in 2008, 'The chal-lenge was to remove the divide so that we have one uniform government.'[6]

In another interview, Bernard Namunane, chief political writer at the *Daily Nation*, added: 'The executive needs to be united, needs cohesion, [and] needs to be reading from one script.'[7] But in the beginning, 'there was no unity, there was no cohesion, and they were not reading from one script'. As soon as Kibaki and Odinga had appointed their cabinet, the president and prime

minister established a joint task force to develop a single coher-
ent policy framework that would guide the work of the coalition
cabinet. The task force was co-chaired by two of the most respected figures in the coalition: Professor Peter Anyang' Nyong'o,
representing the ODM, and Professor George Saitoti, a PNU stal-
wart and cabinet veteran who had once been vice-president.

Together with a group of public servants led by cabinet secretary Francis Muthaura, they started to harmonise the two parties'
campaign manifestos. In an interview with the author, Muthaura
later described this step as 'very important, because [the mani-
festo] was the basis for government policy papers'.[8] According
to Nyong'o, negotiating policy priorities proved to be much less
difficult than anticipated, because 'a number of people in the
coalition, including the prime minister, had also been ministers
in the previous government.'[9] This meant not only that key
members of the two sides were familiar with each other and
with existing cabinet procedures, but also that they could build
on pre-existing policy unity on many issues.

This effort especially benefited from the fact that the previous
government, which included members of both parties, had already managed to reach a degree of consensus around a set of
goals articulated in Vision 2030, a national development strategy
developed with civil society consultation in 2005, similar to South
Africa's National Development Plan. Guided by a detailed set of
policy priorities, the plan aimed to make Kenya a middle-income
country; improve indicators such as health, education, and gen-
der equality; and strengthen democratic institutions.

Aided by the existing consensus around Vision 2030, Muthaura
recalled how the team integrated the two party manifestos into

a single document within 'a matter of one week'.[10] The harmonised manifesto was formally introduced and adopted in June 2008 during a subsequent programme of induction training for ministers. Odinga stressed that that step served to build consensus further, and the fact that the manifesto 'blended the positives of the two documents' meant it was set to 'become the blueprint for the coalition government'.[11]

The adoption of a shared policy agenda at the start of a coalition's term can help to smooth the way for implementation.

Overcoming disagreement

Even with the best-laid plans, disputes are an unavoidable part of coalition governments. Therefore, the strength of a coalition does not necessarily depend on its ability to *avoid* disputes, but on its ability to *manage* them. The GNU and Cape Town cases – as well as Kenya's – point to a number of possible paths to follow in resolving disputes. The first, and perhaps most important, requirement is to make sure that the coalition agreement creates one or more forums that are specifically dedicated to the airing of grievances.

In Cape Town, the seven-party coalition had two forums for resolving disputes. Due to the heavy power imbalance in the coalition, the partners first created a forum that only included the smaller parties – that is to say, it excluded the DA. In her autobiography, Zille acknowledged that: 'At first I thought this was going to be very divisive, but afterwards I realized it was essential for the maintenance of this [coalition]. Because it kept all of the smaller parties believing that they could air their grievances and have a voice, without having to run to the ANC.'[12]

But the coalition deal also included a management committee consisting of all party leaders, including the DA. After the smaller parties had discussed their concerns, they often came to the coalition management committee with a unified position, which enabled them to bargain more effectively with the senior partner. The committee meetings were run according to formal rules and a strict schedule, making it the primary dispute resolution mechanism.

The GNU also provides an example of how to handle policy disputes that cannot be resolved through formal committees. When coalition forums failed to generate consensus on the abolition of the death penalty and the legalisation of abortion, the partners agreed to shift the decisions out of cabinet. Capital punishment was thus handled as a legal matter and referred to the Constitutional Court, where it was abolished. In the case of the disagreement over abortion, the coalition cabinet shifted the debate to Parliament and allowed MPs to vote according to their conscience. In both cases, the coalition avoided deadlock by relying on the judiciary and the legislature.

Coalition management forums and other formal mechanisms are essential parts of any successful coalition government. But they are rarely enough. Another key feature of successful alliances is that they create space for informal methods of conflict resolution. The years of negotiations that preceded the creation of the GNU meant that the leaders of the respective parties had already built inter-personal relationships. As De Klerk recounted, both he and Mbeki often used smoke breaks during cabinet meetings to have one-on-one discussions with ministers who were unhappy about a particular decision. The fact that ANC, NP and IFP ministers had got to know each other during the negotiations to end apartheid helped enormously. But the GNU also relied heavily on Jakes Gerwel, director-general in the president's office. Leaders from all three coalition partners identified Gerwel's measured personality and stature as a respected intermediary as a key factor in overcoming disagreements.

In Cape Town, Zille worked closely with the FF+'s Dirk Smit – the speaker in council – to flag issues that came up during meetings of the smaller parties. In Kenya, Kibaki and Odinga nominated their trusted allies Francis Muthaura and Mohamed Isahakia as lieutenants. Muthaura and Isahakia, who were former colleagues and had an established working relationship, often met behind the scenes to flag and attempt to resolve disputes before they escalated.

According to Isahakia, 'this would involve arranging for the president to meet with the prime minister one-to-one [to] resolve issues that were difficult'.[13] This approach often led to agreement. In creating opportunities for those informal dialogues between the principals, Isahakia emphasised that his 'interaction with Muthaura was always important – sometimes pre-empting potential problems. At times when I sensed there were issues that our side would take a hard position on [that could] then lead into an impasse, I would quietly go and seek an audience with Muthaura.'[14] This private back-channel communication between Kibaki and Odinga also enabled them to present a united front in public and in the cabinet.

Informal back channels are an invaluable way of resolving disputes among coalition partners. In order to work, they often rely on trusted political lieutenants who have pre-existing relationships with people on the other side, and have the emotional intelligence needed to strike compromises before disputes escalate. It is therefore vital to identify the right people with the necessary intuition to smooth relations among the different groups.

In her autobiography, Zille attested to the centrality of relying on people with emotional intelligence and intuitive judgement: 'Coalitions are more vulnerable to issues of style than of substance. During the first year of our term, the size of offices, toilets, cars, drivers, protocol and overseas trips were more frequent topics of contentious debate than major policy decisions.'[15] Nevertheless, she concludes that: 'You can get [coalitions] to work, even a complex coalition, [if leaders and their lieutenants are able to] judge the people, context and issues. So much of leadership is intuition, understanding the variables, reading dynamics accurately. I had to delegate a lot, so putting the right people in the right position is half the problem solved.'[16]

While some decisions ultimately come down to the judgement of the most senior political leaders, the dialogue and compromises engineered by formal coalition management forums, as well as informal backchannels, make them vital tools in the quest to make coalitions cohesive and productive.

Building a coalition culture

Besides the tangible mechanisms that political leaders can put in place to promote the success of coalition governments, there is one additional – and more intangible – factor that often plays a role in shaping the incentives around political coalitions. Although difficult to define, the atmosphere or political culture within which coalition governments operate can have a powerful effect on political leaders' willingness to seek productive compromise.

The GNU is one example of a coalition that operated in a favourable political atmosphere. After decades of mounting fear that South Africa would descend into civil war, the negotiated settlement that resulted in the election of the coalition government led by Nelson Mandela inaugurated a hopeful atmosphere of reconciliation and co-operation. Despite attempts by contemporary reactionaries and revisionists to paint the GNU as an ANC sell-out, the fact is that, at that time, co-operation among political leaders created a positive feedback effect in South African society.

Relieved that the country had averted civil war, and optimistic that the revered Mandela would inaugurate a brighter future, South Africans generally embraced the co-operation and compromises struck among the ANC and its partners. The fanfare that accompanied the adoption of the final Constitution in 1996 – the ultimate expression of inter-group compromise – attested to the approval with which most South Africans regarded the GNU's co-operative work.

Whereas the tireless efforts of people like Archbishop Desmond Tutu and countless other civil society leaders helped to create an atmosphere that was conducive to coalition governance, a country's political culture can also create an environment that is deeply hostile to productive political compromise. As we saw in Chapter Four, Nepal has seen a succession of failed coalition governments. One factor in that country's failure to engineer productive coalitions is undoubtedly the high levels of lingering tension and mistrust among different ethnic and cultural groups involved in the civil war.[17] The never-ending political deadlock in Nepal should serve as an example to revisionist South Africans of what could have happened had there been no concerted effort after the 1994 transition to foster dialogue and reconciliation in a way that promoted tolerance and compromise.

A different example comes from Britain, a country which has a winner-take-all electoral system, and where coalition governments are therefore exceedingly rare. In May 2010, Britain had its first hung Parliament in more than two decades, whereafter the Liberal Democrats entered into a coalition with the Conservatives. It was the first coalition government since 1974 in a country where politics have traditionally been fiercely adversarial. Although the vast majority of the Liberal Democrats' election promises were formally incorporated into the coalition agreement, polls showed that support for the party plummeted immediately after it joined the Conservatives in coalition.[18]

Voters' unease with the Liberal Democrats turned into a full-scale rebellion when the party broke an election promise to oppose higher university fees.[19] The decision to support higher fees essentially ended the career of party leader Nick Clegg, who resigned in 2015 after support for the Liberal Democrats plunged from 57 Parliamentary seats to eight.[20] It was a potent illustration of how a failure to communicate effectively with voters who are not used to the compromise inherent to coalition governance can lead to electoral catastrophe.

On the one hand, these examples illustrate that political leaders continually need to bring their voters along during the coalition journey. It is vital for parties always to communicate publicly *why* compromise on any given decision is important. Rather than striking deals in secret – which inevitably raises suspicions – politicians are well served by communicating openly with the public. No political party can remain in a coalition without some level of buy-in from its supporters.

At the same time, party leaders will also face the challenge of bringing their own caucuses along on the coalition journey. In their interviews, both De Klerk and Zille stressed that some of the strongest resistance to compromise came from within their own parties. It is thus vital for parties to communicate to their rank and file about the reasons for any controversial decisions taken in the interest of strengthening cross-party co-operation, as internal political opponents are likely to use such compromises to attack party leaders.

But fostering a political and public ethos that is amenable to the compromises required by coalition governance is not only the responsibility of elected leaders. Civil society organisations, universities, as well as individual citizens have a tremendously important role to play in facilitating better relations among the supporters of different parties.

In the wake of the favourable atmosphere that supported the work of the GNU, South Africans have largely allowed civic engagement to collapse. Ironically, the ANC's hegemony since 1994 has been one of the key causes of civic apathy, as voters have outsourced their agency to a domineering political party. Besides ending the ANC's dominance, South Africans also need to rediscover their spirit of civic engagement. Although the 2017 protests against the Zuma administration was a hopeful sign, civil society and citizens need to engage more actively in the search for progressive solutions to the country's many challenges. It is only through engaging with problems, and with one another, that voters will help generate the incentives for political coalitions to be both cohesive and productive.

Conclusion

Having covered the *why*, *what* and *how* of South Africa's coalition future, all that remains is to predict which of our three scenarios are most likely to be realised should the ANC lose power in 2019. In this conclusion, I will also assess whether South Africa is ready to meet the unprecedented demands that coalitions will impose on political leaders and citizens alike.

In terms of the ability to assemble and manage coalition governments, the DA has a head start over its rivals. Unlike other established opposition parties such as the UDM, IFP and FF+, the DA has grown consistently over the past decade, which has made it the senior partner in a number of coalition governments.

Of all South African parties, the DA has by far the most experience when it comes to striking coalition deals. As the recent cases in Cape Town and Nelson Mandela Bay have shown, DA leaders are also able to keep coalitions together through turbulent times. Given its long life, and relatively extensive governing experience, the DA has developed significant institutional memory. Moreover, its sophisticated and competent in-house leadership training team means the DA is also well positioned to translate its institutional memory into training programmes for its public representatives, thereby preparing the party for leading coalitions from 2019 onwards.

Although the EFF lacks institutional memory, it has also participated in a number of coalition negotiations since its formation in 2013. While it did not enter any formal coalitions after the 2016 elections, it has co-operated with the DA through its agreement to support DA-led minority governments in Johannesburg and Tshwane. However, given the party's relative youth and its personalisation of power, it has not yet developed the sophisticated training systems needed to build a cohort of effective negotiators and managers. Beyond the small clique of leaders around Julius Malema, most EFF representatives are not well versed in the complexities of coalition management.

As the coalition era draws near, the ANC may soon find that its domination of South African politics since 1994 has been a double-edged sword. With nearly unfettered power over the last two-and-a-half decades, the ANC has never truly *needed* coalition partners. While it co-operated effectively with the NP and IFP in the GNU, it was never entirely dependent on those parties to remain in power. In other places where the ANC has attempted to govern through coalitions, such as the Western Cape and KwaZulu-Natal, the alliances have not lasted for long, and have achieved very little.

In what should serve as a clear warning sign to party leaders, the ANC has been unable to convince any of South Africa's major opposition parties to co-operate with it after the 2016 municipal elections. Apart from disbursing patronage, the ANC clearly lacks the institutional capacity to negotiate effectively with other parties. The problem has been aggravated by the brain drain that weakened the party after Zuma came to power in 2007, as most of the remaining Mbeki-aligned officials who were active in the GNU were pushed out.

Despite these variations among the major parties, it is safe to say that all South African political parties still have a long way to go in building the expertise they need to manage governing coalitions. Ours has been a one-party state ever since the transition to democracy, with all the hardened attitudes and partisanship that go with political domination. Building the more co-operative inter-party relations required for coalitions to work will take time, but political parties can overcome their differences if they believe this is in their best interests.

A greater cause for concern is that, at precisely the moment when South Africa needs to build a coalition culture, social attitudes appear to be hardening. Unlike the atmosphere of reconciliation when the GNU came to power, South Africa's next national coalition government will grapple with a more intransigent and divided society.

Alarmingly, the strongest example of how tolerance, compromise and inter-group dialogue have retreated in South Africa comes from university campuses. This is where fundamentalists like the Fallist movement are socialising the next generation of influential middle-class voices and voters. Although the student protests ignited by the #RhodesMustFall and #FeesMustFall movements in 2015 initially showed promise by uniting students around demands to lower unaffordable tuition fees, the Fallist movement quickly degenerated into violent riots, and assumed a racist, proto-fascist character.

In 2016, the Fallists rampaged across university campuses, causing more than R600 million in damages.[1] University administrators were desperate to end the violence, and often agreed to meet even the most outrageous and ill-defined student demands. But the Fallist leaders at most universities kept moving the goalposts, and refused to compromise or strike deals with university managements. Just a short period before the crucial 2019 election that could inaugurate the coalition era in South African politics, many reactionary university students are still rejecting all forms of compromise as a 'sell-out'.

The radicalisation of university campuses is a worrying development. We have already seen how the EFF in particular has attempted to actively associate with the Fallists, but it will surely not be the only party that seeks to appease this newly influential social group. For most of 2016, the Fallists were perhaps the biggest media story in the country, and no political party wants to miss out on that kind of attention. The danger is that, in this new atmosphere of zero-sum citizenship, parties will shun compromise and co-operation for fear of being labelled as sell-outs by radical yet influential voices.

But the Fallist fundamentalists could probably not have risen without the help of the social media. Alongside the rise of Fallism, then, the influence of social media on the country's politics poses another threat to South Africa's coalition future. When websites like Facebook and Twitter were first popularised in the late 2000s, most observers welcomed them as tools that would democratise access to information and cross-fertilise political debates by enabling people with different political views to engage in robust dialogue. By allowing people from different sides of the political spectrum to easily talk to one another, it was hoped that these tools would foster greater understanding, empathy, and co-operation across political boundaries.

In South Africa – as in most countries – the opposite is happening. The algorithms used by websites like Facebook tend to steer users towards content aligned with their existing ideological preferences.[2] These algorithms understand that users are more likely to engage with content that confirms what they already believe, which means that Facebook and Twitter purposefully expose its users to content they literally 'like', while shielding them from opinions that do not fit their online identity.

This problem is exacerbated by the advent of fake news websites. They are generally created by two kinds of people. The first group is motivated by profit. Because online advertising services like Google AdSense pay websites for every click they generate, these fake news entrepreneurs write false yet provocative stories aimed at specific users whom they know will click on the alluring headlines. With every click on a fake news story, the website owner makes money.

This phenomenon has been powerfully illustrated by the emergence of so-called troll farms in countries like Macedonia on the Balkan Peninsula in Eastern Europe, where thousands of mostly teenagers wrote fake pro-Donald Trump stories in the lead-up to the 2016 US election.[3] The authors of fake news articles like 'Pope Francis shocks world, endorses Donald Trump for president'[4] did not generally create those fabrications because they supported Trump – they mostly did it because they knew millions of Trump-supporting Facebook users would click on the headline, generating thousands of dollars in advertising revenues.

While the 2016 US election campaign is the most high-profile example of the impact of troll farming to date, no democracy is immune to it. South Africa has already witnessed the rise of fake news websites such as 'African News Updates' and 'CitySun', which post links on Facebook and Twitter in the hope of attracting clicks.[5]

But there is a second group of fake news purveyors that is arguably even more dangerous than the troll farmers, who are largely motivated by profit. This second group of online fraudsters is motivated by political goals. The most high-profile example also comes from the 2016 US presidential election, during which the Russian government posted at least 3 000 political advertisements on Facebook with the explicit goal of influencing the American electorate in favour of Donald Trump. An estimated 10 million Americans were exposed to these ads, which often contained outright lies about Trump's opponents in both the Republican and Democratic parties.[6]

In 2017, a similar story played itself out in South Africa. The role played by the UK-based public relations firm Bell Pottinger in manufacturing fake news aimed at discrediting opponents of the corrupt Gupta family is a textbook case of how social media are being exploited to polarise South Africa. Bell Pottinger worked with Zuma and Gupta acolytes to create a false narrative that agents of 'white monopoly capital' had fabricated the corruption allegations against Zuma and the Guptas. The campaign demonised racial minorities, and purposefully sought to exploit racial divisions in order to distract attention from the real crimes of the Zuma-Gupta cabal.

Although massive public pressure eventually forced Bell Pottinger out of business, local social media networks remain littered with 'Guptabots' – fake accounts that continue to spread propaganda aimed at inciting hatred towards minorities and those fighting back against Zuma's state capture.[7] Amid mounting evidence that the Russian state is interfering in elections around the world,[8] South Africans can also expect a barrage of online pro-ANC propaganda during the 2019 election campaign, as Russian president Vladimir Putin seeks to protect the R1 trillion nuclear deal allegedly struck with ANC leaders.

While the motives of Macedonian teenagers might be different from those of Russian hackers and Gupta trolls, the impact on democracy and cross-party compromise is equally devastating. The algorithms used by social media websites confine users to political and ideological echo chambers, where they are almost exclusively exposed to content that reinforces their existing political beliefs. Worse still, purveyors of fake news exploit the same social media algorithms to expose users to outright lies about people with different political persuasions, driving internet users deeper into the deceptive safety of their respective echo chambers.

As a result, instead of building bridges among people as was initially hoped, social media have reinforced the political barriers among different groups. Websites like Twitter and Facebook have helped to ensure that supporters of the ANC, DA, and EFF inhabit different political realities, and the social media outrage machine now almost entirely defines the parameters of political debate in South Africa.

This has already had real-world consequences. While, in a 2017 report, the Institute of Race Relations found that the country's racial fabric is still mostly 'sound', it also warned that 'that fabric is also now fraying . . . If this negative trend persists over a number of years, our current social fabric could fray to a disturbing degree.'[9] Along similar lines, Afrobarometer has found that South Africans have become less willing to obey the laws of a government they did not vote for. Between 2005 and 2015, it reports, the percentage of people who said they would not obey a government they did not support jumped from 12 per cent to 18.6 per cent.[10]

The rise of proto-fascist Fallism that rejects all forms of compromise, enabled by and combined with the construction of ideological echo chambers by the social media, has already deeply divided South Africa. As the economy continues to decline, it is likely that social relations – especially along racial lines – will become even more strained. In the run-up to the 2019 election, it will therefore be more important than ever to guard against the type of political extremism that rejects all compromise and inter-group co-operation.

Institutions like universities can make a valuable contribution to the cause of building a coalition culture by urgently ramping up leadership and negotiation training for its students, while civil society groups should organise debates and round tables about the implications of political coalitions. South Africans should also become more aware of how fake news and social media biases are creating artificial divisions among groups which might otherwise be willing to hammer out mutually beneficial compromises.

More than anything, the future of coalition politics rests with South African voters. This book has attempted to start a discussion among voters about what the end of ANC hegemony and the onset of coalition government are likely to mean. The good news is that we don't need to wait for politicians, universities, or civil society groups to prepare us for the coming coalition era.

As citizens, we need to start thinking about the strategic implications of our votes. Which political parties are likely to team up in our municipality? What are the values we want coalitions to be built upon? What are the issues we are willing to compromise on, and in exchange for what? Should we be loyal to only one political party, or would coalitions at different levels of government be better served if we split our votes among different parties? And since relatively small parties will soon play an outsized role in our politics, should we start thinking more about forming new parties if we don't like the existing options? It is only through constant discussion and debate with our families, friends, colleagues, and communities that we will begin to overcome the radicalism engineered by those who would see us divided, and instead build the culture of dialogue, compromise, and mutually beneficial co-operation that will play a key role in making coalitions work.

But South Africa still has a long way to go towards fostering a coalition culture. Given that most political parties are still unprepared for coalitions, and that attitudes are hardening, working against compromise and co-operation in the process, the most likely outcome of coalition negotiations should the ANC lose its majority in 2019 is that of a minority government. This is the option that came about in the hung councils of Johannesburg and Tshwane after the ANC had lost its majorities in those metros in 2016. As discussed in Chapter Seven, this scenario is likely to lead to the election of a DA-led cabinet that does not have a legislative majority, and is hamstrung by its constant fight to build cross-party legislative support.

Under a minority government, voters should be prepared for a bumpy ride. Stories about political intrigue and backstabbing would dominate the media, as parties try to build fresh majorities for every piece of legislation. Without a stable majority government in place, opposition party leaders would have little incentive to compromise with a minority cabinet. Motivated exclusively by self-interest, they would approach every legislative proposal with the question: 'What's in it for us?'

With no coalition agreement in place to articulate shared values among different parties, legislative alliances would be fluid and opportunistic. For example, while the ANC and EFF could support a DA bill to increase social grants and overhaul the wasteful South African Social Security Agency (SASSA), they could team up the next day to block the DA's proposed land laws, and enact expropriation without compensation. In such a situation, it would become extremely difficult to understand the country's overall policy direction in areas like education and health care, as shifting allegiances would produce a mish-mash of different laws.

More worryingly, a deadlocked legislature could lead to pork-barrel politics. In order to garner enough legislative support for its agenda, a minority government would need to provide tangible benefits to opposition parties. Those attempts to 'sweeten the deal' could well mean that corruption would be spread among most parties. But it would be a different kind of graft from the type that devoured the ANC. When it was the only game in town, the ANC did not need to clear room at the trough for other parties; corruption was almost exclusively an ANC phenomenon.

Under a minority government, corruption would probably re-volve less around a single party, and more around the exchange of political favours among different parties.

The instability inherent to minority governance could even lead to a government shut-down. Since opposition lawmakers would outnumber those from the governing DA, nothing would prevent the EFF, ANC and other parties from banding together and remov-ing the minority cabinet through a vote of no confidence that would only require a majority of 50 per cent plus one. If Parlia-ment was unable to reconstitute a cabinet, this could even mean that the country will need to hold early elections. Although this would be an extreme move likely to provoke public protests, it would be a real risk as long as political leaders were unable to assemble a majority coalition.

Despite these risks, there is also a potential upside to the minority government scenario. In an effort to circumvent the deadlock in Parliament, a DA-led cabinet would probably rely far more heavily on the substantial executive powers vested in the president by the Constitution. Free from the constraint of having to appease a formal coalition partner, in areas where the cabinet has significant say – such as economic and foreign policy – the DA would probably be able to implement significant parts of its agenda. In turn, South Africa could experience something of an economic revival, while its standing among the world's liberal democracies would improve.

But the reforms would probably not go deep enough. Without dependable support in Parliament, the government would not be able to fundamentally alter the status quo. Although moderate economic growth would return, the unemployment and crime rates would not decrease substantially. Inequality would probably increase marginally as skilled people with access to capital reaped the benefits of a stronger economy, while those at the bottom remain locked out by still-broken education and health care systems. Corruption would persist, albeit at lower levels and in a different shape than under the ANC. Under the most likely scenario of a minority government, the ship of state would be guided into calmer waters, but would not yet be turned around.

The second most likely scenario is that contemplated in Chapter Five, of a formal DA-EFF coalition that would also include smaller parties like the ACDP, COPE, IFP, FF+ and UDM, and perhaps an ANC splinter party. Should leaders of these parties rise above the increasingly vitriolic fray of the country's public debate to strike a formal deal based on shared constitutional values, this scenario presents a decidedly more optimistic picture than the go-slow of minority government.

Despite the obvious ideological differences between the DA and EFF, these parties have shown a surprising willingness to cooperate since the 2016 municipal elections. However, they would need to deepen their relations even further if they are to form a formal alliance government after the 2019 election. The sheer scale of this challenge is what makes this a less likely scenario than a minority government. But while sealing a coalition deal would be a tall order, the payoffs for South Africa could be significant.

With a formal agreement in place, the DA-EFF cabinet would not be subject to the type of deadlock and insecurity that is sure to dog any minority government. Rather than publicly negotiating each and every piece of legislation in Parliament, party leaders could use internal forums to iron out policy details and resolve disputes before publicly introducing joint proposals. By creating a shared agenda that emphasises commonality rather than difference, by creating joint oversight over ministerial portfolios, and through continual back-channel communication between party leaders, a formal DA-EFF coalition could engineer fruitful compromises that would benefit all citizens.

The single most important reform likely to emerge from such a partnership is an end to cadre deployment, and the creation of a fit-for-purpose civil service. Even if it wanted to, a minority government would not have the legislative power to bring about such a fundamental change, while any alternative coalition arrangement that involved the ANC would never willingly dismantle its own corruption empire. Only a DA-EFF coalition would potentially have the political will and the Parliamentary numbers to begin to unravel the web of graft and state capture that has brought the country to its knees.

The DA's sober and more market-oriented economic policies also have the potential to eliminate government wastage and improve the business environment, thereby unleashing the full potential of South Africa's entrepreneurs, creating millions of new job opportunities, and ultimately lowering poverty. In turn, the EFF may push the government towards a greater focus on expanding social programmes, and reducing inequality. A DA-EFF alliance is thus the only coalition configuration with the potential to begin to fix South Africa. A minority government is more likely, but if these two parties do manage to fuse their policies pragmatically, it could bring out the best in both, and create a coalition government that would be greater than the sum of its parts.

While an ANC-EFF coalition is the least likely of the three scenarios, it will be important to keep an eye on Julius Malema's conduct and statements in the run-up to the 2019 elections. We cannot entirely discount the possibility that Malema might want to return to the ANC. In late 2017, in an address filled with his usual racist vitriol, Malema even went as far as to say that the EFF's relationship with the DA was like dating someone after breaking up 'with your real lover', and that the party would only work with the DA while looking for its 'real lover'.[11] If the EFF is indeed playing the long game, with its eye on ultimately gaining control of the ANC, South Africa's economy and democracy would be in even deeper trouble.

In contrast to a DA-EFF coalition, a governing alliance between the ANC and EFF would probably bring out the worst in both parties. The relationship between the ANC and EFF is based on grievances and on settling old scores – the very founding of the EFF in 2013 was in retaliation for Malema having lost a factional fight against Jacob Zuma. It is therefore highly unlikely that an ANC-EFF coalition would be based on shared constitutional values, with the aim of bringing about a better South Africa. Instead, it would be based on the ANC's desperate need to hang on to power at any cost, and the EFF's desire to win the populist battle it started in the late 2000s.

With the ANC totally unprepared for the coalition era, the EFF would try to exact one concession after another. Populists within the ANC, including the women's league, youth league, and the so-called premier league leaders from the Free State, North West and Mpumalanga, would probably jump on the 'expropriation without compensation' bandwagon. Although opposition parties

241

and civil society would fight back, the country would start living in a populist and socialist nightmare.

The civil service would be stripped of its last remaining skills as cadre deployment was entrenched to allow the EFF to join the looting. As schools and hospitals collapsed amid the brain drain, the ANC-EFF coalition would probably pull all the populist school leavers at its disposal: It could hike the minimum wage to unsustainable levels, and health care as well as education at all levels could be declared free overnight, wiping out the remaining pockets of excellence in the private sector, and ensuring that all citizens had access to equally poor services. When the economy would inevitably begin to implode, as investors fled the country, the populist gang could emulate its role models in Venezuela and Zimbabwe, printing money and scapegoating ethnic minorities by expropriating private land, mines, and companies to feed their insatiable hunger for looting state assets.

After inheriting an already sinking economy from Jacob Zuma, the populist coalition could trigger the greatest economic crisis in modern South African history. As the economy worsened, violent crime would probably spike to unprecedented levels. Facing an increasingly desperate population caught in the grip of skyrocketing inflation, economic implosion, and a fraying social fabric, the ANC-EFF coalition might clamp down on civic, judicial, and media freedoms. Within the span of one electoral term, a populist coalition could bring South Africa's economy and democracy to the verge of collapse. An ANC-EFF coalition is the least likely of the three scenarios. But if it comes to pass, South Africa's first democratically elected coalition government could also be its last.

If political leaders and voters alike shun compromise and co-operation, the country will end up with an unstable minority government that tries to fix problems with one hand tied behind its back. Conversely, if politicians and citizens create an environment that is conducive to cross-party co-operation and compromise based on the values articulated in the Constitution, coalitions have the potential to produce tremendous shared economic and social progress. However, if political leaders opt for coalition compromises that are based purely on expediency and unconstitutional populist impulses, South Africans are sure to pay a heavy price.

Regardless of which of the three scenarios ultimately comes to pass, coalition governance will profoundly change South Africa. After seven decades of being ruled by a single party – the NP between 1948 and 1994, and the ANC since 1994 – the country stands on the cusp of a fundamental transformation that will usher in an era of multiparty governance.

Quite soon, voters will determine whether the coalition era dawns in 2019, or whether its arrival will be postponed. Therefore, the fundamental question confronting voters in the 2019 elections will be whether to preserve the ANC's dominant majority, or hand the keys to a national coalition government. (At the provincial level, they will also determine whether Gauteng, North West and the Northern Cape get coalition governments.) To answer this question, South Africans will need to compare the three coalition scenarios outlined in this book with what the country and its provinces will look like if the ANC alone remains in power.

During the past two-and-a-half decades, voters have lived through the ANC's descent into maladministration and corruption, and it is difficult to see how re-electing the party for five more years will magically stop the bleeding. In the end, handing the ANC another dominant majority in 2019 could be just as disastrous as an ANC-EFF coalition. Under an all-powerful ANC, South Africa is already on the road to disaster. While an (unlikely) coalition partnership with the EFF might add some rhetorical and ideological fireworks to the journey, Jacob Zuma's presidency has made it clear that the ANC is perfectly capable of crippling the country on its own, without the assistance of the Malema brigade.

For example, whereas an ANC-EFF coalition might expropriate private property after 2019 under the guise of populist, socialist ideological conviction, a still-dominant ANC might do the same in an effort to keep its looting going and hand more property to the likes of the Guptas. The reasons might look different, but the outcome would be equally as disastrous for regular citizens. Therefore, preserving the ANC's domination might be just as bad as the worst-case (and most unlikely) coalition scenario.

For the ANC, the most optimistic scenario is that the new leadership elected in December 2017 will slow the country's decline. This is essentially what some ANC members promised prior to the 54th National Conference when they spoke about the party 'self-correcting'.[12] In the current context of institutionalised looting, it would indeed be a tragic achievement for this hollowed-out party if it could contain corruption and maladministration at present levels, and perhaps even prosecute some of the lower-level thieves. But even leaders who promise 'self-correction' realise that it is near-impossible for the ANC actually to address the country's structural problems.

Even the most ardent ANC supporters would quietly concede

that the best a new ANC administration could do would be to slow down – not stop – the decline. The corruption and decay is too deep, too fundamental, and too much a part of the party's DNA for the ANC to return the country to the path of prosperity. The ANC alone cannot fix South Africa. At worst, another ANC majority will see it rapidly destroying what is left of the economy. At best, it will more slowly destroy what is left of the economy.

Even the middling coalition scenario of minority government is likely to achieve more than an ANC majority that somehow manages to 'self-correct'. Put differently, even if Ramaphosa appointed all the capable people left in the ANC to cabinet, another single-party ANC administration would still be less effective than a DA-led minority government. This is because the new ANC leadership would be hamstrung by the need to hold the divided party together.

The war waged by Jacob Zuma's storm troopers against Thabo Mbeki at the ANC's 2007 Polokwane conference cracked the ANC like an eggshell. Those fissures widened during the Zuma presidency, as cadres competed for room at the trough while a minority of reform-minded party members looked on in horror. A decade after the cracks first appeared, they have grown into chasms. In 2013, in a previously unthinkable move, a group of trade unions led by the powerful National Union of Metalworkers of South Africa (NUMSA) resigned from Cosatu, and left the ANC alliance.[13] The SACP has similarly threatened to leave the alliance and run against the ANC in 2019,[14] while the divisions between the Zuma-aligned premier league and Ramaphosa supporters were starkly visible in the lead-up to the December 2017 conference.

These divides will not disappear, and will prevent the ANC from changing course. Should the party retain its majority in 2019, the new administration will soon find that any meaningful reform proposal will be stymied by the networks of corrupt politicians and bureaucrats put in place by cadre deployment. The different constituent parts of the ideologically confused tripartite alliance will continue to pursue its own agendas, leading to the same type of inertia that allowed Zuma and the Guptas to continue looting with impunity long after their crimes had first been exposed. The ANC is paralysed, and no matter how many members may yearn to walk again, the party's spinal cord cannot be re-grown.

Given these deep internal divisions, any new ANC administration would be even more deadlocked than a DA-led minority government. While a minority government would be slowed down by the need to constantly build and rebuild majorities whenever it wanted to change a law, the DA would have significant power to enact executive policy changes that do not require Parliamentary approval – for the simple reason that, unlike the ANC, the party is not at war with itself. Ironically, the ANC's internal civil war has escalated to the point where, even if the party gains another majority in 2019, it will not be able to use that tremendous power to implement difficult reforms – even if it wanted to.

The implication is that, in 2019, both a minority government *and* a DA-EFF coalition would be better for South Africa than even the most well-intentioned ANC single-party government, while the worst possible ANC government would be just as destructive as a populist ANC-EFF coalition. Given that an ANC-EFF alliance is the *least* likely outcome of coalition negotiations, South Africa's future would probably be in safer hands if no single party gets 50 per cent in 2019.

Besides potentially putting the country back on a path to prosperity, the onset of the coalition era in 2019 would also finally fulfil the Constitution's vision of creating a coalition-based society based on proportional representation. The transition to inclusive democracy meant that most closed and authoritarian apartheid-era state institutions, including the rules for running elections, were replaced with the open and inclusive institutions needed to run a diverse society anchored in liberal democracy. When leaders of different parties designed the country's Constitution in the mid-1990s, they deliberately chose an electoral system that would put as many voices as possible in Parliament, while forcing different parties to co-operate and compromise if no single party got 50 per cent of the vote.

Despite the adoption of the proportional representation system, single-party domination survived the transition to democracy. For two-and-a-half decades, the ANC's extraordinary popularity has allowed it to override the need for coalitions. But as the ANC pushes South Africa closer to the brink, and as the attraction of its liberation narrative fades while opposition parties continue to make electoral gains, the era of single-party domination is drawing to a close. For South Africa to have a shot at salvaging the dream of a future that is brighter than a dark past and gloomy present, ANC domination must urgently be replaced by the compromise and co-operation of coalitions.

Endnotes

INTRODUCTION

1   *Mail & Guardian*, 'Zuma: The ANC will rule till Jesus comes back', 8 January 2014, at http://mg.co.za/article/2014-01-08-zuma-the-anc-will-rule-forever, last accessed on 1/5/2016.

2   Reuters, 'South Africa's rand hits 2-1/2 year high on bets on leadership change', 28 December 2017, at https://af.reuters.com/article/africaTech/idAFKBN1EM0HU-OZABS, last accessed on 10/1/2018.

3   M Mngadi, 'Zuma laughed when the ANC lost metros in the elections – Makhosi Khoza', News24, 30 November 2017, at https://www.news24.com/SouthAfrica/News/zuma-laughed-when-the-anc-lost-metros-in-the-elections-makhosi-khoza-20171130, last accessed on 10/1/2018.

CHAPTER ONE

1   As defined by the Economist Intelligence Unit's 2015 Democracy Index. This figure includes countries designated as 'full democracies' and 'flawed democracies'.

2   All election data cited in this book has been drawn from the IEC database at www.elections.org.za.

3   Interestingly, the NP government that was formed after the 1948 election started out as a coalition of sorts between the Herenigde Nasionale Party (Reunited National Party) and the smaller Afrikaner Party. The two groups formally merged in 1951 to form the NP.

4   Hermann Giliomee, 'South Africa's Emerging Dominant-Party Regime, *Journal of Democracy*, 9 (4), October 1998, 128-142; H Giliomee and C Simkins, *The Awkward Embrace: One-Party Domination and Democracy in Industrialising Countries,* Harwood Academic Publishers, Amsterdam, 1999; M Woollacott, 'The greatest threat to the ANC is its own dominance', *The Guardian*, 15 April 2004, at http://www.theguardian.com/world/2004/apr/16/southafrica.comment, last accessed on 4/5/2016.

5   Note that the projections beyond 2016 (indicated by dashed lines) are not necessarily predictions of what *will* happen in future elections. Instead, they

use a simple algorithm to calculate the statistically most likely outcome of those elections.

6   T Lodge, 'How the South African Electoral System was Negotiated', *Journal of African Elections*, 2 (1), 2003, 71-76, at https://www.eisa.org.za/pdf/JAE2.1Lodge.pdf, last accessed on 15/4/2017.

7   Under winner-take-all systems such as Britain's, the country is divided into different geographic districts. Voters in each district then directly elect a delegate from their region to go to the national Parliament. However, a major drawback of this model is that it does not represent the interests of all, or even most, voters. If party A's candidate in any given district gets 40 per cent of the vote while party B's candidate gets 35 per cent and party C's gets 25 per cent, then only party A's candidate will go to Parliament even though 60 per cent of voters did *not* vote for her. In this example, 60 per cent of the votes will effectively have been wasted.

8   Government of South Africa, Constitution of the Republic of South Africa, Section 46(6), 2 August 2012, at http://www.gov.za/DOCUMENTS/CONSTITUTION/constitution-republic-south-africa-1996-1, last accessed on 29/10/2017.

9   Lodge, 'How the South African Electoral System was Negotiated'.

10 News24. 'EFF: We are the government in waiting', 13 February 2014, at http://www.news24.com/elections/news/eff-we-are-the-government-in-waiting-20140213l, last accessed on 30/4/2017.

11 Deutsche Welle, 'Observers give thumbs up to South Africa's election', 8 May 2014, at http://www.dw.com/en/observers-give-thumbs-up-to-south-africas-election/a-17621136, last accessed on 16/5/2016.

12 N Shange, 'ConCourt gives IEC 18 months to fix voters' roll', News24, 14 June 2016, at http://www.news24.com/elections/news/concourt-gives-iec-18-months-to-fix-voters-roll-20160614, last accessed on 4/4/2017.

13 Helen Suzman Foundation, 'Can the ANC win the Western Cape?', 1 October 2009, at http://hsf.org.za/resource-centre/focus/issue-16-fourth-quarter-1999/can-the-anc-win-the-western-cape, last accessed on 15/5/2016.

14 B Jooste and D Knoetze, 'ANCYL charged after threat to make DA turf ungovernable', *Pretoria News*, 2 August 2012, at http://www.iol.co.za/pretoria-news/ancyl-charged-after-threat-to-make-da-turf-ungovernable-1355187, last accessed on 4/4/2017.

15 *Sunday Times*, 'In Pictures: Blood as chaos erupts at NMB council meeting', 28 October 2016, at http://www.timeslive.co.za/sundaytimes/stnews/2016/10/28/In-Pictures-Blood-as-chaos-erupts-at-NMB-council-meeting, last accessed on 4/4/2017; T Madia, ANC to blame for chaos at JHB council meeting –

Mashaba, News24, 23 February 2017, at http://www.news24.com/SouthAfrica/News/anc-to-blame-for-chaos-at-jhb-council-meeting-mashaba-20170223, last accessed on 4/4/2017; eNCA, 'Tshwane council meeting plunged into chaos', 27 September 2016, at http://www.enca.com/south-africa/tshwane-council-meeting-plunged-into-chaos, last accessed on 4/4/2017.

16   A Saba, L Feltham and K Rupiah, 'Explore SA's killing fields: An interactive map of all 2016 political assassinations', *Mail & Guardian*, 2 August 2016, at https://mg.co.za/data/2016-08-02-explore-sas-killing-fields-an-interactive-map-to-all-political-killings-in-2016, last accessed on 4/4/2017.

CHAPTER TWO

1   T Gqirana, '"Painful" Nelson Mandela Bay has ANC looking at coalitions to retain power', News24, 5 August 2016, at http://www.news24.com/elections/news/painful-nelson-mandela-bay-loss-has-anc-looking-at-coalitions-to-retain-power-20160805, last accessed on 2/4/2017.

2   eNCA, 'DA-led coalition fears governing party interference', 18 August 2016, at http://www.enca.com/south-africa/da-led-coalition-fears-governing-party-interference, last accessed on 19/09/2017.

3   C Gould, C Barberton, and C Adboll, 'What is at stake for new councils in South Africa?', *ISS Today,* Institute for Security Studies, 17 August 2016, at https://issafrica.org/iss-today/what-is-at-stake-for-new-councils-in-south-africa, last accessed on 2/4/2017.

4   Ibid.

5   Ibid.

6   The rollup of municipal results indicated here only include the proportional representation ballots, and exclude the direct ward ballots. This is because proportional voting is a more valid way of comparing municipal results with national results, as national elections only use proportional voting.

7   eNCA, 'The state of SA according to grant beneficiaries', 31 March 2017, at http://www.enca.com/south-africa/do-not-publish, last accessed on 3/4/2017.

8   Afrobarometer, 'In South Africa, citizens' trust in president, political institutions drops sharply', *Dispatch 90*, 17 May 2016, at http://Afrobarometer.org/sites/default/files/publications/Dispatches/ab_r6_dispatchno90_south_africa_trust_in_officials.pdf, last accessed on 3/4/2017.

9   Ipsos, 'Majority of ANC members say Zuma must resign, 30 May 2017, at https://www.ipsos.com/en-za/majority-anc-members-say-zuma-must-resign, last accessed on 9/6/2017.

10 This figure has been calculated for analytical purposes and is not an official election result. The 54.49 per cent is calculated by adding together all of the proportional representation votes that the ANC received in municipalities during the 2016 municipal elections.

11 CNN, Christiane Amanpour interviews Pravin Gordhan, at https://www.youtube.com/watch?v=rt6Pi34dm3M, last accessed on 4/5/2017.

12 Z George, 'ANC could lose 2019 elections, warns Chief Whip Jackson Mthembu', *Dispatch Live*, 24 March 2017, at http://www.dispatchlive.co.za/featured/2017/03/24/anc-could-lose-2019-elections-warns-chief-whip-jackson-mthembu/, last accessed on 4/5/2017.

13 S Grootes, 'ANC will have to perform miracle to obtain 50% in 2019', *Eyewitness News*, 20 February 2017, at http://ewn.co.za/2017/02/20/anc-will-have-to-perform-miracle-to-obtain-50-in-2019, last accessed on 4/5/2017; Huffington Post South Africa, 'Work hard now or lose Gauteng in 2019, Mashatile warns ANC', 5 February 2017, at http://www.huffingtonpost.co.za/2017/02/05/work-hard-now-or-lose-gauteng-in-2019-mashatile-warns-anc/, last accessed on 4/5/2017; R Masego, 'Mashatile: ANC no longer a leader', *Eyewitness News,* 3 May 2017, at http://ewn.co.za/2017/05/03/paul-mashatile-says-anc-losing-ground, last accessed on 4/5/2017; A Deklerk, 'Unite or we will lose power in 2019: ANC treasurer-general Zweli Mkhize', 1 May 2017, TimesLive, at http://www.timeslive.co.za/politics/2017/05/01/Unite-or-we-will-lose-power-in-2019-ANC-treasurer-general-Zweli-Mkhize1, last accessed on 4/5/2017; H Nhlabathi, Sisulu slams ANC decay, News24, 23 April 2017, at http://www.news24.com/SouthAfrica/News/sisulu-slams-anc-decay-20170423-3, last accessed on 4/5/2017.

14 SA Breaking News, 'Motlanthe not sure he can vote ANC in 2019', 26 April 2017, at http://www.sabreakingnews.co.za/2017/04/26/motlanthe-not-sure-he-can-vote-anc-in-2019/, last accessed on 4/5/2017.

15 S Daley, 'South Africa scandal over "Sarafina" spotlights corruption in the ANC', *New York Times*, 8 October 1996, at http://www.nytimes.com/1996/10/08/world/south-africa-scandal-over-sarafina-spotlights-corruption-in-the-anc.html, last accessed on 6/5/2017.

16 A Feinstein, 'Bright hopes betrayed', *The Guardian*, 10 January 2007, https://www.theguardian.com/commentisfree/2007/jan/10/somethingisrotten, last accessed on 6/5/2017.

17 702, 'Seriti Commission on arms deal – R113 million later – finds no wrong-doing', 21 April 2016, at http://www.702.co.za/articles/13046/arms-deal-

commission-finds-no-evidence-of-wrongdoing-an-activist-reacts, last accessed on 6/5/2017.

18   *Mail & Guardian*, 'NPA drops corruption charges against Zuma', 6 April 2009, at https://mg.co.za/article/2009-04-06-npa-drops-corruption-charges-against-zuma, last accessed on 6/5/2017.

19   T Petersen, 'Cosatu gives Dlamini a week to resign or face "massive protest"', News24, 12 March 2017, at https://www.news24.com/SouthAfrica/News/cosatu-gives-dlamini-a-week-to-resign-or-face-massive-protest-20170312, last accessed 10/12/2017.

20   amaBhungane, '#GuptaLeaks: Duduzane Zuma's UAE residency confirmed', 3 June 2017, at http://amabhungane.co.za/article/2017-06-03-guptaleaks-duduzane-zumas-uae-residency-confirmed, last accessed on 9/6/2017; M Wa Afrika and S Hofstatter, 'Inside Zuma's Dubai palace . . . and Mugabe lives next door', *Sunday Times*, 4 June 2017, at http://www.timeslive.co.za/sundaytimes/stnews/2017/06/04/Inside-Zumas-Dubai-palace-...-and-Mugabe-lives-next-door, last accessed on 9/6/2017.

21   AmaBhungane and Scorpio, 'How Eskom was captured', Daily Maverick, 9 June 2017, at https://www.dailymaverick.co.za/article/2017-06-09-amabhungane-and-scorpio-guptaleaks-how-eskom-was-captured/#.WTqYocYlHIU, last accessed on 9/6/2017; TimesLive, 'Gupta associates scored billions in kickbacks from Transnet deals, 1 June 2017, at http://www.timeslive.co.za/politics/2017/06/01/Gupta-associates-scored-billions-in-kickbacks-from-Transnet-deals-report, last accessed on 9/6/2017.

22   L Grant, 'Infographic: Poverty in South Africa', *Mail & Guardian*, 5 February 2015, at https://mg.co.za/data/2015-02-05-infographic-poverty-in-south-africa, last accessed on 6/5/2017.

23   Afrobarometer, 'Handling managing the economy', Round 6, 2014/2015, at http://www.Afrobarometer.org/online-data-analysis/analyse-online, last accessed on 6/5/2017.

24   L Peyper, 'Recovery from junk status will take 7 years – economist', Fin24, 3 June 2016, at http://www.fin24.com/Economy/recovery-from-junk-rating-will-take-7-years-economist-20160603, last accessed on 6/5/2017.

25   Gareth Newham, 'A case of poisoned chalice or poisoned politics?', Institute for Security Studies, 6 June 2017, at https://issafrica.org/iss-today/a-case-of-poisoned-chalice-or-poisoned-politic, last accessed on 9/6/2017.

26   Ibid.

27   Ibid.

28   Statistics South Africa, *Victims of Crime Survey 2015/16,* at http://www. statssa.gov.za/publications/P0341/P03412015.pdf, last accessed on 9/6/2017.

CHAPTER THREE

1   H Zille, 'The Cape Town Story', Politicsweb, 28 March 2011, at http://www. politicsweb.co.za/party/the-cape-town-story–helen-zille, last accessed on 20/4/2017.

2   S Hlongwane, 'DA launches its Cape Town Story', Daily Maverick, 28 March 2011, at https://www.dailymaverick.co.za/article/2011-03-28-da-launches-its-cape-town-story#.WPkcXallHIV, last accessed on 20/4/2017.

3   G Van Onselen, 'Bankruptcy stalks Nelson Mandela Bay', *Financial Mail,* 13 February 2017, at https://www.businesslive.co.za/fm/features/2017-02-10-bankruptcy-stalks-nelson-mandela-bay/, last accessed on 20/4/2017; *Pretoria News,* 'Msimanga set to bring change to Tshwane', 5 September 2016, at http://www.iol.co.za/pretoria-news/opinion/msimanga-set-to-bring-change-to-tshwane-2064720, last accessed on 20/4/2017; S Hlongwane, 'City of fraudsters: the Auditor-General's horror report on Johannesburg', Daily Maverick, 27 February 2013, at https://www.dailymaverick.co.za/article/2013-02-27-city-of-fraudsters-the-Auditor-Generals-horror-report-on-johannesburg/#.WPkhHallHIU, last accessed on 21/4/2017.

4   Statistics South Africa, *Labour Force Survey,* March 2017, at http://www. statssa.gov.za/publications/P0210/P0210March2007.pdf, last accessed on 21/4/2017.

5   Statistics South Africa, *Millennium Development Goals – Goal 2,* 2013, at http://www.statssa.gov.za/MDG/MDG_Goal2_report_2013.pdf, last accessed on 21/4/2017.

6   Statistics South Africa, *Census 2011 In Brief,* at http://www.statssa.gov.za/census/census_2011/census_products/Census_2011_Census_in_brief. pdf, last accessed on 21/4/2017.

7   Ipsos, 'Profiles of the supporters of the three biggest political parties in South Africa', November 2013, at http://www.ipsos.co.za/SitePages/Profiles %20of%20the%20supporters%20of%20the%20three%20biggest%20 political%20parties%20in%20South%20Africa.aspx, last accessed on 21/4/2017.

8   Ibid.

9   H Giliomee, 'South Africa's Emerging Dominant-Party Regime', *Journal of Democracy,* 9 (4): 128-142.

CHAPTER FOUR

1   R Hopper, 'Post apartheid South Africa: evaluating South Africa's institutional design', *Opticon* 1826, 5, 2008, at http://ojs.lib.ucl.ac.uk/index.php/up/article/view/1426, last accessed on 25/06/2017.

2   A Lijphart, 'South African democracy: Majoritarian or consociational?' *Democratization*, 5 (4), 1998, 144-150, at http://www.tandfonline.com/doi/abs/10.1080/13510349808403588, last accessed on 25/06/2017.

3   Ibid.

4   Ibid.

5   L A Schreiber, '"Reconciling the impossible": South Africa's Government of National Unity, 1994-1996', *Innovations for Successful Societies,* Princeton University, 2016, at http://successfulsocieties.princeton.edu/sites/success fulsocieties/files/LS_POWERSHARING_South%20Africa_ FORMATTED_19Dec2016_0.pdf, last accessed on 25/06/2017.

6   FW de Klerk, 'Statement by Mr FW De Klerk, leader of the National Party', Nelson Mandela Centre of Memory, 1996, at https://www.nelsonmandela.org/omalley/index.php/site/q/03lv02039/04lv02046/05lv02047/06lv02049/07lv02064.htm, last accessed on 25/06/2017.

7   C Sunstein, *Designing Democracy: What Constitutions Do,* Oxford University Press, 2001.

8   World Bank, 'GDP Growth (annual %)', 2017, at http://data.worldbank.org/indicator/NY.GDP.MKTP.KD.ZG?locations=ZA, last accessed on 25/06/2017.

9   Public Service Commission. *Public Service Commission Report on the Rationali sation of Public Administration in the Republic of South Africa, 1994-1996.* 1996.

10   Schreiber, 'Reconciling the impossible'.

11   Ibid.

12   T Eloff, 'Another national unity government?', IOL News, 18 March 2017, at http://www.iol.co.za/news/opinion/another-national-unity-government-8244885, last accessed on 25/06/2017; J Rossouw, 'South Africa will need a government of national healing after Zuma leaves', The Conversation, 12 June 2017, at http://theconversation.com/south-africa-will-need-a-government-of-national-healing-after-zuma-leaves-79063, last accessed on 25/06/2017.

13   United Nations Development Programme, *Human Development Report 2016,* 21 March 2017, at http://hdr.undp.org/sites/default/files/2016_human_development_report.pdf. Last accessed on 25/06/2017.

14   J Hellström, 'There are important differences between coalition formation processes in West European and Central/East European states', London

School of Economics and Political Science, 13 August 2014 at http://blogs.lse. ac.uk/europpblog/2014/08/13/there-are-important-differences-between-coalition-formation-processes-in-west-european-and-centraleast-european-countries/, last accessed on 30/08/2017.

15   D R Henderson, 'German Economic Miracle', *Concise Encyclopaedia of Economics, Library of Economics and Liberty,* at http://www.econlib.org/library/ Enc/GermanEconomicMiracle.html, last accessed on 30/08/2017.

16   H C Wallich, *Mainsprings of the German Revival,* New Haven: Yale University Press, 1955, at http://www.econlib.org/library/Enc/GermanEconomicMiracle. html.

17   W Chughtai, 'Berlin Wall: German reunification "a success story"', CBC News, 9 November 2014, at http://www.cbc.ca/news/world/berlin-wall-german-reunification-a-success-story-1.2828271, last accessed on 31/08/2017.

18   All Indian election results cited in this book are drawn from the website http://www.elections.in/, last accessed on 31/08/2017.

19   World Bank, 'GDP growth (annual %)'.

20   Author's calculations, based on World Bank, 'GDP growth (annual %)'.

21   Substantial parts of this discussion of Kenya's coalition politics were first published in L A Schreiber, 'Making power sharing work: Kenya's grand coalition cabinet, 2008-2013', *Innovations for Successful Societies*, Princeton University, September 2015, at http://successfulsocieties.princeton. edu/sites/successfulsocieties/files/LS_Kenya_Powersharing_FINAL.pdf, Last accessed on 31/08/2017.

22   M Wrong, *It's Our Turn to Eat: The Story of a Kenyan Whistle-Blower*, Harper, New York, 2010.

23   International Crisis Group, *Kenya in Crisis*, Africa Report No 137, 21 February 2008.

24   Ibid.

25   Ibid.

26   See UK Department for International Development, 'Elections in Kenya in 2007', 14 March 2016, at https://www.gov.uk/government/uploads/system/ uploads/attachment_data/file/67654/elections-ke-2007.pdf, last accessed on 31/08/2017; also see internaldisplacemenet.org at http://www.internaldisplace-ment.org/sub-saharan-africa/kenya/figures-analysis. These numbers are lower than some of those initially announced; for example, see BBC News, 'Kenya rivals agree to share power', 28 February 2008, at http://news.bbc.co.uk/ 2/hi/africa/7268903.stm, last accessed on 31/08/2017.

27 Kenya National Dialogue and Reconciliation Monitoring Project, *Progress Review Report,* March 2012, at http://www.south.co.ke/images/south/KNDR_ Reports/14thReviewReportMarch2012.pdf, last accessed on 31/08/2017.

28 Ipsos Public Affairs, *Political Barometer Survey,* 25 January 2013, at http:// www.nation.co.ke/blob/view/-/1674940/data/453146/-/d6mapaz/-/Ipsos. pdf, last accessed on 31/08/2017.

29 Substantial parts of this discussion on Nepal's coalition politics were first published in L A Schreiber, 'Escaping Political Deadlock: Nepal's Caretaker Cabinet, 2013-2014', *Innovations for Successful Societies,* Princeton University, February 2016, at https://successfulsocieties.princeton.edu/sites/success- fulsocieties/files/LS_Nepal_Powersharing_Final.pdf, last accessed on 31/08/2017.

30 BBC News, 'Nepal raises conflict death toll', 22 September 2009, at http:// news.bbc.co.uk/2/hi/8268651.stm, last accessed on 31/08/2017.

CHAPTER FIVE

1 News24, 'Zuma scolds "clever" blacks', November 2012, at http://www.news24. com/Archives/City-Press/Zuma-scolds-clever-blacks-20150429, last accessed on 01/07/2017.

2 News24, 'Nomvula Mokonyane's "dirty votes" comment angers Bekkersdal', 25 October 2013, at http://www.news24.com/Archives/City-Press/Nomvula- Mokonyanes-dirty-votes-comment-angers-Bekkersdal-20150429, last accessed on 01/07/2017.

3 G Quintal, 'The ANC comes first, not the country – Zuma', News24, 8 No- vember 2015, at http://www.news24.com/SouthAfrica/News/the-anc-comes- first-not-the-country-zuma-20151108, last accessed on 01/07/2017.

4 H Nhlabath, 'We can't think "coalition" – that's defeatist, says ANC's Mthe- thwa', *City Press,* 4 July 2017, at http://city-press.news24.com/News/we-cant- think-coalition-thats-defeatist-says-ancs-mthethwa-20170704, last accessed on 27/07/2017.

5 eNCA, 'Mashaba for mayor still an issue for Malema', 18 August 2016, at http://www.enca.com/south-africa/mashaba-for-mayor-still-a-sticking- point-for-malema, last accessed on 27/07/2017.

6 Democratic Alliance, *Vision 2029: Maximising Service Delivery by Minimis- ing Cabinet,* February 2016, at https://www.da.org.za/wp-content/uploads/ 2016/02/Vision-2029-Maximising-Service-Delivery-by-Minimising-Cabinet- correct-version.pdf, last accessed on 15/09/2017.

7 Politicsweb, 'How the ANC politicised the state', 7 April 2009, at http://www.

politicsweb.co.za/news-and-analysis/how-the-anc-politicised-the-state. last accessed on 15/09/2017.

8   H Bhorat, K Naidoo and K Pillay, 'South Africa's civil servants are the country's new labour elite', The Conversation, 19 February 2016, at http://theconversation.com/south-africas-civil-servants-are-the-countrys-new-labour-elite-54269, last accessed on 01/07/2017.

9   A Breytenbach and J Rossouw, ''n Ontleding van vergoedingsneigings in die Suid-Afrikaanse staatsdiens, 2005 tot 2012', Tydskrif vir Geesteswetenskappe, 53 (4), December 2013, at http://www.scielo.org.za/pdf/tvg/v53n4/11.pdf, last accessed on 01/07/2017.

10   J Rossouw, 'Civil service pay: South Africa has some harsh choices to make', The Conversation, 29 January 2016, at http://theconversation.com/civil-service-pay-south-africa-has-some-harsh-choices-to-make-53389, last accessed on 01/07/2017.

11   Fin24, 'SA's debt to GDP highest among emerging market peers – report', 26 September 2016. At https://www.fin24.com/Economy/sas-debt-to-gdp-highest-among-emerging-market-peers-report-20160926, last accessed on 04/11/2017.

12   Democratic Alliance, DA Policy on Governance, December 2013, at http://www.da.org.za/wp-content/uploads/2014/01/Governance1.pdf, last accessed on 01/07/2017; Julius Sello Malema, 'Manifesto: Our plans for local govt – EFF', Politicsweb, 4 May 2016, at http://www.politicsweb.co.za/documents/manifesto-our-plans-for-local-govt–eff, last accessed on 01/07/2017.

13   A Visser, 'NHI costs to skyrocket', Business Report, 1 July 2016, at https://www.iol.co.za/business-report/economy/nhi-costs-to-skyrocket-2040660, last accessed on 15/09/2017.

14   The Economist, 'South Africa has one of the world's worst education systems', 7 January 2017, at https://www.economist.com/news/middle-east-and-africa/21713858-why-it-bottom-class-south-africa-has-one-worlds-worst-education, last accessed on 13/08/2017.

15   M Cohen, 'SA spends higher proportion of budget on education than US, UK', Fin24, January 2017, at http://www.fin24.com/Economy/sa-spends-more-on-education-than-us-uk-and-germany-20170105, last accessed on 13/08/2017.

16   V John, 'With grade R comes great responsibility', Mail & Guardian, 14 August 2015, at https://mg.co.za/article/2015-08-14-with-grade-r-comes-great-responsibility, last accessed on 15/09/2017.

17   Department of Basic Education, *Report of the ministerial task team appointed by minister Angie Motshekga to investigate allegations into the selling of posts of educators by members of teachers unions and departmental officials in provincial educations departments,* 25 May 2016, at https://nicspaull.files.wordpress.com/2016/05/dbe-2016-volmink-report.pdf, last accessed on 16/08/2017.

18   C Walker and A Dubb, *The Distribution of Land in South Africa: An Overview,* Institute for Poverty, Land and Agrarian Studies, 2013, http://www.plaas.org.za/sites/default/files/publications-pdf/No1%20Fact%20check%20web.pdf, last accessed on 13/08/2017.

19   M Noble, W Zembe and G Wright, 'Poverty may have declined, but deprivation and poverty is still worst in the former homelands', Econ3x3, 27 May 2014, at http://www.econ3x3.org/article/poverty-may-have-declined-deprivation-and-poverty-are-still-worst-former-homelands, last accessed on 13/08/2017.

20   EFF, 'Policy on land', at http://www.effonline.org/on-land, last accessed on 13/08/2017.

21   L A Schreiber, 'Land rights in the township: Building incremental tenure in Cape Town, South Africa, 2009-2016', *Innovations for Successful Societies,* Princeton University, February 2017, at https://successfulsocieties.princeton.edu/sites/successfulsocieties/files/LS_Land_SouthAfrica_May2017.pdf, last accessed on 20/08/2017.

22   Statistics South Africa, *Community Survey 2016,* at http://cs2016.statssa.gov.za/wp-content/uploads/2016/07/NT-30-06-2016-RELEASE-for-CS-2016-_Statistical-releas_1-July-2016.pdf, last accessed on 20/08/2017.

23   Politicsweb, 'Manifesto: Our plans for local govt – EFF', 4 May 2016, at http://www.politicsweb.co.za/documents/manifesto-our-plans-for-local-govt–eff, last accessed on 20/08/2017.

24   S Graham, 'Manyi under fire for coloured remarks', *Mail & Guardian,* 24 February 2011, at https://mg.co.za/article/2011-02-24-manyi-under-fire-for-coloured-remarks, last accessed on 18/08/2017.

25   P De Vos, 'Manyi was just being honest', Constitutionally Speaking, 24 February 2011, at http://constitutionallyspeaking.co.za/manyi-was-just-being-honest/, last accessed on 16/08/2017.

26   World Bank, *Doing Business Index 2009,* at http://www.doingbusiness.org/~/media/WBG/DoingBusiness/Documents/Annual-Reports/English/DB09-FullReport.pdf, last accessed 20/08/2017; World Bank, *Doing Business Index*

2017, at http://www.doingbusiness.org/data/exploreeconomies/south-africa, last accessed on 20/08/2017.

27   World Bank, 'GDP per capita, PPP (constant 2011 $ international), 2017, at http://data.worldbank.org/indicator/NY.GDP.PCAP.PP.KD?locations=ZA, last accessed on 28/08/2017.

CHAPTER SIX

1   N Goba, 'Julius Malema will not go back to the ANC, says the EFF's Mbuyiseni Ndlozi', *Business Day*, 13 March 2017, at https://www.businesslive.co.za/bd/politics/2017-03-13-julius-malema-will-not-go-back-to-the-anc-says-the-effs-mbuyiseni-ndlozi/, last accessed on 22/08/2017.

2   D Hawker, 'Stakes high in Malema case', eNCA, 2 August 2015, at http://www.enca.com/south-africa/stakes-high-malema-case, last accessed on 15/08/2017.

3   IOL News, 'Malema's properties to be auctioned', 21 February 2013, at https://www.iol.co.za/news/crime-courts/malemas-properties-to-be-auctioned-1474239, last accessed on 25/08/2017.

4   eNCA, 'Massive increase in irregular expenditure by government: AG', at https://www.enca.com/south-africa/massive-increase-in-irregular-expenditure-by-government-ag, last accessed on 04/11/2017.

5   IOL News, 'R1 trillion nuclear deal will guarantee SA junk status', 9 April 2017, at https://www.iol.co.za/news/politics/r1-trillion-nuclear-deal-will-guarantee-sa-junk-status-8565844, last accessed on 30/08/2017.

6   H Zille, *Not Without a Fight: The Autobiography,* Cape Town: Penguin Random House, 2016.

7   Z George and S Ford, 'ANC call for Bay to be put under administration "bid to take back metro"', DispatchLive, 31 August 2017, at http://www.dispatchlive.co.za/politics/2017/08/31/anc-call-bay-put-administration-bid-take-back-metro/, last accessed on 11/09/2017.

8   *Mail & Guardian,* 'Zuma: The ANC will rule till Jesus comes back', 8 January 2014, at http://mg.co.za/article/2014-01-08-zuma-the-anc-will-rule-forever, last accessed on 1/5/2016.

9   World Bank, 'GDP per capita, PPP (constant 2011 $ international), 2017', at http://data.worldbank.org/indicator/NY.GDP.PCAP.PP.KD?locations=ZA, last accessed on 28/08/2017.

CHAPTER SEVEN

1   South African Government, Constitution of the Republic of South Africa, 1996, Section 79: Assent to Bills, at http://www.gov.za/DOCUMENTS/CONSTITUTION/constitution-republic-south-africa-1996-1, last accessed on 28/08/2017.

2   World Bank, 'Doing Business Index 2017', at http://www.doingbusiness.org/data/exploreeconomies/south-africa, last accessed on 20/08/2017.

3   A Khoza, 'South Africa should have arrested Al-Bashir – ICC', News24, at http://www.news24.com/SouthAfrica/News/south-africa-failed-to-arrest-al-bashir-icc-20170706, last accessed on 29/08/2017.

4   BBC News, 'Grace Mugabe: South Africa grants immunity despite assault claim', 20 August 2017, at http://www.bbc.com/news/world-africa-40990934, last accessed on 29/08/2017.

5   Y Groenewald, 'The state of renewable energy in SA', *City Press*, 16 February 2016, at http://city-press.news24.com/Business/the-state-of-renewable-energy-in-sa-20160216, last accessed on 29/08/2017.

6   Democratic Alliance, *Towards 2029: The DA's 5-Point 'Jobs' Plan for Economic Freedom, Fairness and Opportunity,* at http://www.da.org.za/wp-content/uploads/2015/08/The-DAs-5-Point-Jobs-Plan.pdf, last accessed on 29/08/2017.

7   World Bank, 'GDP per capita, PPP (constant 2011 $ international), 2017', at http://data.worldbank.org/indicator/NY.GDP.PCAP.PP.KD?locations=ZA, last accessed on 28/08/2017.

CHAPTER EIGHT

1   B Keller, 'Mandela Completes His Cabinet, Giving Buthelezi a Post', *New York Times,* 12 May 1994, at http://www.nytimes.com/1994/05/12/world/mandela-completes-his-cabinet-giving-buthelezi-a-post.html?mcubz=1, last accessed on 04/09/2017.

2   The chapter on the GNU coalition is a shortened version of L A Schreiber, '"Reconciling the Impossible": South Africa's Government of National Unity, 1994-1996', *Innovations for Successful Societies,* Princeton University, December 2016, at http://successfulsocieties.princeton.edu/sites/successfulsocieties/files/LS_POWERSHARING_South%20Africa_FORMATTED_19Dec2016_0.pdf, last accessed on 04/09/2017.

3   South African Government, Constitution of the Republic of South Africa, Act 2000 of 1993, section 88 (4), at http://www.gov.za/documents/constitution/constitution-republic-south-africa-act-200-1993, last accessed on 04/09/2017.

4   Ibid.

5   FW de Klerk, *The Autobiography: The Last Trek, a New Beginning,* Canopus Consultancies, Cape Town, 1994.

6   FW de Klerk, interview with the author, Cape Town, 7 October 2016.

7   Ibid.

8   Ibid.

9   S Mufamadi, interview with the author, Johannesburg, 3 October 2016.

10   S Du Plessis and B Smit, 'South Africa's Growth Revival after 1994', Stellenbosch Economic Working Paper: 01/06, March 2007, at https://core.ac.uk/download/pdf/6358779.pdf, last accessed on 04/09/2017.

11   Mufamadi, interview.

12   Mufamadi, interview.

13   South African History Online, '1994 Cabinet', at http://www.sahistory.org.za/article/1994-cabinet, last accessed on 04/09/2017.

14   G Aboobaker, interview with the author, Cape Town, 25 October 2016.

15   R Meyer, interview with the author, Stellenbosch, 30 September 2016.

16   De Klerk, interview.

17   A Kathrada, interview with the author, Cape Town, 7 October 2016.

18   Meyer, interview.

19   De Klerk, *Autobiography*.

20   Ibid.

21   Mufamadi, interview.

22   De Klerk, interview.

23   B Fanaroff, interview with the author, Cape Town, 28 September 2016.

24   Meyer, interview.

25   S Bitar and A F Lowenthal (eds), 'Interview with President Thabo Mbeki', in *Democratic Transitions: Conversations with World Leaders*, International Institute for Democracy and Electoral Assistance, 2015.

26   South African Government, Constitution of the Republic of South Africa, section 89 (3).

27   Meyer, interview.

28   Bitar and Lowenthal (eds), 'Interview with President Thabo Mbeki'.

29   De Klerk, interview.

30   Aboobaker, interview.

31   L Wessels, 'Negotiations, GNU, power-sharing, and post-conflict reconstruction in South Africa, in D Kotzé and H Solomon (eds), *The State of Africa:*

Post-conflict Reconstruction and Development, Africa Institute of South Africa, Pretoria, 2008.

32 N Haysom, interview with the author, 6 October 2016.

33 Wessels, 'Negotiations'.

34 Haysom, interview.

35 De Klerk, *Autobiography*.

36 Ibid.

37 Wessels, 'Negotiations'.

38 J Gerwel, interview with Padraig O'Malley, O'Malley Archive, 8 November 1994, at https://www.nelsonmandela.org/omalley/index.php/site/q/03lv00017/04lv00344/05lv00832/06lv00862.htm, last accessed on 05/09/2017.

39 De Klerk, *Autobiography*.

40 De Klerk, interview.

41 De Klerk, *Autobiography*.

42 Ibid.

43 Ibid.

44 Ibid.

45 Mufamadi, interview.

46 De Klerk, *Autobiography*.

47 Ibid.

48 Meyer, interview.

49 Bitar and Lowenthal, 'Interview with President Thabo Mbeki'.

50 De Klerk, *Autobiography*.

51 'Statement by Mr FW de Klerk, Leader of the National Party', O'Malley Archive, 9 May 1996, at https://www.nelsonmandela.org/omalley/index.php/site/q/03lv02039/04lv02046/05lv02047/06lv02049/07lv02064.htm, last accessed on 05/09/2017.

52 Ibid.

53 Ibid.

54 'Statement by President Nelson Mandela on the National Party's withdrawal from the Government of National Unity (GNU)', Nelson Mandela Foundation, 9 May 1996, at http://www.mandela.gov.za/mandela_speeches/1996/960509_np.htm, last accessed 05/09/2017.

55 Haysom, interview.

56 A Eveleth, 'Inkatha could leave GNU after poll', *Mail & Guardian*, 28 June 1996, at http://mg.co.za/print/1996-06-28-inkatha-could-leave-gnu-after-poll, last accessed on 05/09/2017.

CHAPTER NINE

1   G Nicolson, 'ANC takes back Mogale City amid controversy', Daily Maverick, 29 June 2017, at https://www.dailymaverick.co.za/article/2017-06-29-anc-takes-back-mogale-city-amid-controversy/#.Wa0jVdFLe00, last accessed on 04/09/2017.

2   R de Kock, 'Nelson Mandela Bay council removes Bobani as deputy mayor', TimesLive, 24 August 2017, at https://www.timeslive.co.za/politics/2017-08-24-nelson-mandela-bay-council-removes-bobani-as-deputy-mayor/, last accessed on 04/09/2017.

3   S Grootes, 'Analysis: Coalition governments – nigh impossible, but may be SA's only good option', Daily Maverick, 28 August 2017, at https://www.dailymaverick.co.za/article/2017-08-28-analysis-coalition-governments-nigh-impossible-but-may-be-sas-only-good-option/, last accessed on 04/09/2017.

4   G Van Onselen, 'Anatomy of a coalition coup: Are there lessons ahead of the August election?', *Business Day*, 11 July 2016, at https://www.business-live.co.za/bd/opinion/columnists/2016-07-11-anatomy-of-a-coalition-coup-are-there-lessons-ahead-of-the-august-election/, last accessed on 05/09/2017.

5   South African Government, Municipal Structures Act 117 of 1998, at https://www.gov.za/sites/default/files/a117-98_0.pdf, last accessed on 06/09/2017.

6   Van Onselen, 'Anatomy of a coalition coup'.

7   Ibid.

8   Ibid.

9   Ibid.

10 Ibid.

11 Ibid.

12 Zille, *Not Without a Fight*.

13 H Zille, interview with the author, Cape Town, 25 July 2017.

14 Ibid.

15 Van Onselen, 'Anatomy of a coalition coup'.

16 Ibid.

17 Ibid.

18 Ibid.

19 Zille, *Not Without a Fight*.

20 Ibid.

21 Zille, interview.

22 Ibid.

23 Ibid.

24 M Woldemariam, 'Municipal Turnaround in Cape Town, South Africa, 2006-

2009', *Innovations for Successful Societies,* Princeton University, March 2011, at https://successfulsocieties.princeton.edu/sites/successfulsocieties/files/Policy_Note_ID162.pdf, last accessed on 07/09/2017.

25 Ibid.

26 Ibid.

27 Zille, interview.

28 Ibid.

29 Ibid.

30 Ibid.

31 Ibid.

32 Zille, *Not Without a Fight.*

33 Ibid.

34 Zille, interview.

35 Zille, interview.

36 Ibid.

37 Ibid.

38 Ibid.

39 Ibid.

40 *Mail & Guardian,* 'Major blow for DA's Cape Town coalition', 16 January 2007, at https://mg.co.za/article/2007-01-16-major-blow-for-das-cape-town-coalition. last accessed on 08/09/2017.

41 Woldemariam, 'Municipal Turnaround in Cape Town'.

42 Ibid.

CHAPTER TEN

1 K Ngoepe, 'ANC takes Joburg, but gets below 50%', News24, 6 August 2016, at http://www.news24.com/elections/news/anc-gets-below-50-in-joburg-20160806, last accessed on 11/09/2017.

2 RTL Nieuws, 'Zo werkt de kabinetsformatie: praten, verkennen en formeren', 16 March 2017, at https://www.rtlnieuws.nl/nieuws/laatste-videos-nieuws/zo-werkt-de-kabinetsformatie-praten-verkennen-en-formeren, last accessed on 11/09/2017.

3 South African Government, Municipal Structures Act.

4 L A Schreiber, 'Making Power Sharing Work: Kenya's Grand Coalition Cabinet, 2008-2013', *Innovations for Successful Societies,* Princeton University, September 2015, at http://successfulsocieties.princeton.edu/sites/successfulsocieties/files/LS_Kenya_Powersharing_FINAL.pdf, last accessed on 12/09/2017.

5 Van Onselen, 'Anatomy of a coalition coup'.

6   Raila Odinga, interview with the author, Nairobi, 15 September 2015.

7   Bernard Namunane, interview with the author, Nairobi, 17 September 2015.

8   Francis Muthaura, interview with the author, Nairobi, 18 September 2015.

9   P A N'yongo, interview with the author, Nairobi, 16 September 2015.

10 Muthaura, interview.

11 Odinga, interview with the author, Nairobi, 15 September 2015.

12 Zille, *Not Without a Fight*.

13 M Isahakia, interview with the author, Nairobi, 25 September 2015.

14 Ibid.

15 Zille, *Not Without a Fight*.

16 Ibid.

17 Fox News World, 'Ethnic divides underlie Nepal's political divides, 31 May 2012, at http://www.foxnews.com/world/2012/05/31/ethnic-divides-underlie-nepal-political-turmoil.html, last accessed on 14/09/2017.

18 *Evening Standard*, 'Lib-Dem conference to attack school reforms', 10 August 2010, at https://web.archive.org/web/20110107025337/http://www.thisis-london.co.uk/standard/article-23865334-coalition-under-pressure-as-liberal-democrat-support-plummets.do, last accessed on 14/09/2017.

19 BBC News, 'Tuition fees vote: Plans approved despite rebellion', 9 December 2010, at http://www.bbc.co.uk/news/uk-politics-11952449, last accessed on 14/09/2017.

20 M Weaver, 'Nick Clegg's tuition fees "debacle" undermined trust, says Norman Lamb', *The Guardian*, 12 May 2015, at https://www.theguardian.com/politics/2015/may/12/nick-clegg-university-tuition-fees-norman-lamb, last accessed on 14/09/2017.

CHAPTER ELEVEN

1   BusinessTech, 'Damage to SA universities hits R600 million – and counting', 27 September 2016, at https://businesstech.co.za/news/government/138169/damage-to-sa-universities-hits-r600-million-and-counting/, last accessed on 12/09/2017.

2   NPR.org, 'The Reason Your Feed Became An Echo Chamber – And What To Do About It', 24 July 2016, at http://www.npr.org/sections/alltechconsidered/2016/07/24/486941582/the-reason-your-feed-became-an-echo-chamber-and-what-to-do-about-it, last accessed on 04/11/2017.

3   Wired, 'The Macedonian Teens Who Mastered Fake News', 15 February 2017,

at https://www.wired.com/2017/02/veles-macedonia-fake-news/, last accessed on 04/11/2017.

4   FactCheck.org, 'Did the Pope Endorse Trump?', 24 October 2016, at http://www.factcheck.org/2016/10/did-the-pope-endorse-trump/, last accessed on 04/11/2017.

5   eNCA, 'Ten fake news sites to be wary of', 23 January 2017, at https://www.enca.com/south-africa/fake-news-sites-to-watch-out-for-on-the-net, last accessed on 04/11/2017.

6   D Byers, 'Facebook: Russian ads reached 10 million people', CNN, 3 October 2017, at http://money.cnn.com/2017/10/02/media/facebook-russian-ads-10-million/index.html, last accessed on 04/11/2017.

7   K Child, 'Pro-Gupta bots unmasked', TimesLive, 10 July 2017, at https://www.timeslive.co.za/politics/2017-07-10-pro-gupta-bots-unmasked/, last accessed on 04/11/2017.

8   O Dorell, 'Alleged Russian political meddling documented in 27 countries since 2004', *USA Today*, 7 September 2017, at https://www.usatoday.com/story/news/world/2017/09/07/alleged-russian-political-meddling-documented-27-countries-since-2004/619056001/, last accessed on 04/11/2017.

9   South African Institute of Race Relations, 'Sound but fraying at the edges', February 2017, at http://irr.org.za/reports-and-publications/occasional-reports/files/race-relations-in-south-africa-2013-reasons-for-hope-2017, last accessed on 12/09/2017.

10   Afrobarometer, 'Obey government always vs. only if vote for it', Round 6, 2014/2015, at http://www.Afrobarometer.org/online-data-analysis/analyse-online, last accessed on 6/5/2017.

11   N Marrian, 'EFF could ditch DA if Cyril Ramaphosa wins', *Business Day*, 3 November 2017, at https://www.businesslive.co.za/bd/opinion/columnists/2017-11-03-natasha-marrian-eff-could-ditch-da-if-cyril-ramaphosa-wins/, last accessed on 04/11/2017.

12   N Goba, 'ANC will "self-correct" at its December conference, says Mantashe', *Business Day*, 24 October 2017, at https://www.businesslive.co.za/bd/politics/2017-10-24-anc-will-self-correct-at-its-december-conference-says-mantashe/, last accessed on 29/10/2017.

13   L Polgreen, 'South Africa's Biggest Trade Union Pulls Its Support for ANC', *New York Times*, 20 December 2013, at http://www.nytimes.com/2013/12/21/world/africa/south-africas-biggest-union-pulls-support-for-anc.html?_r=0, last accessed on 29/10/2017.

14   eNCA, 'SACP to go it alone in elections', 15 July 2017, at https://www.enca.com/south-africa/sacp-to-go-it-alone-in-elections/, last accessed on 29/10/2017.

Acknowledgements

The inspiration for this book grew over a number of years as I travelled around the world to conduct research on cases of successful government reform. During hundreds of interviews with government officials championing reforms in dozens of developing countries, the importance of building and maintaining political coalitions repeatedly emerged as vitally important. This exposure to diverse political contexts played a key role in helping me to understand how unique – and ultimately unsustainable – democratic South Africa's situation of one-party domination under a proportional representation framework truly was.

While the ideas and arguments discussed in this book are my own, I am deeply grateful to Professor Jennifer Widner, Pallavi Nuka, Doug Hulette, and the rest of the fantastic team of scholars at Princeton University's Innovations for Successful Societies programme for granting me this exposure to new places, people and ideas. I also wish to thank them for helping me hone my analytical and writing abilities over the years I have worked there, and for allowing me a month away from work to complete the manuscript.

Although I had begun scribbling some notes on what the seemingly inevitable shift to coalition governance could mean for South Africa, this book would not have happened without the support and dedication of publisher Maryna Lamprecht and the excellent team at Tafelberg. Their professionalism and trust in my abilities kept me on track while tackling this daunting challenge. Special thanks also goes to Erika Oosthuysen, head of non-fiction at Tafelberg, who first approached me about writing this book, and to my data wizard friend Aldu Cornelissen for helping make the graphics readable. I am equally grateful to all the interviewees who took precious time to speak with me about their experiences of, and expectations for, South Africa's coalition future.

The unwavering support and enthusiasm of my family was of inestimable value, especially on days when it seemed like an overly ambitious task to complete the manuscript on a part-time basis in only seven months. I am eternally grateful to my parents, Johann and Suma, for their open-minded and unqualified support for my endeavours, as well as to my brothers, Harold and Hanno, for their examples of hard work and perseverance. A final word of thanks goes to my fiancée, Julia, whose intelligence, curiosity, and unwavering empathy helped carry this project to completion.

Leon Schreiber
January 2018

Index

Page numbers in *italics* refer to figures.

About the author

DR LEON SCHREIBER is a Senior Research Specialist at the Innovations for Successful Societies programme at Princeton University in the United States, conducting research on how to build effective and accountable government institutions in developing countries.

Prior to joining Princeton in 2015, he obtained a PhD in Political Science *magna cum laude* from the Free University of Berlin, Germany, as well as MA, BA (Honours) and BA degrees from Stellenbosch University.

In 2015 he was the runner-up in the prestigious St. Gallen Symposium Wings of Excellence award for future leaders, and in 2017 he was selected by the *Mail & Guardian* as one of the Top 200 Young South Africans.

After studying and working abroad for five years, Schreiber moved back to Cape Town in 2016. Besides his work for Princeton, he regularly participates in television and radio programmes as a political analyst, writes for some of South Africa's leading newspapers and magazines, and tends to his vegetable garden.